VANABODE

Vanabode allows you to travel further, easier, cheaper,
and for longer periods of time, than any other method of travel.
You will see more for less, day after day, year after year,
than you ever thought possible.

D1455889

Table of Contents

Online Travel Destinations http://www.vanabode.com/travel/destinations.htm) covers where to go, what to see, pictures, advice, weather, expected budget, and more.

Using This Book

In order to keep the book to a reasonable size I could not embed *all* the pictures, maps, and information. If I had, the book would be over 1,600 pages long. To see the rest of it, visit the links *included in the book*. These links will take you to the *Vanabode store* where you can purchase equipment or other books, to the *Destinations Guide* containing our personal travel diaries with 1,000's of pages of travel advice and hundreds of pictures showing where we recommend you go and where we recommend you do not go, to the *Forum* so you can meet other travelers and get more help, to the *Make Money* page listing hundreds of job opportunities updated daily, and to the *Links* page where you get a list of the most important travel resources, other than this book, in one place.

Most of these links included in the book are currently NOT reachable from the normal Vanabode website but are created especially for buyers of the book only. These resources are updated constantly, another reason their individual content could not be included in the actual book. I have instead provided links to pages on my website *that contain all the additional current information you need* to support your new travels.

If you purchased a version of Vanabode *OTHER* than the PDF version directly from my website; (like Kindle users or printed book buyers), contact me immediately using my email address (http://www.vanabode.com/contact.htm). Tell me your email address and request the special instructions and latest links to pages **NOT** found in the book itself. I will then send you information available ONLY to buyers of the book and links to *pages that cannot be reached from the regular Vanabode website.*

I want to support all Vanabode customers. Your questions, comments, trip reports, corrections, and criticism are all important to me. Use the Vanabode Forum or email me.

Jason Odom

Vanabode Overview

Anybody can live an exciting, fun, and very romantic life using the Vanabode techniques and tools found in this book. There are hundreds of variables in each person's life creating millions of specific sets of circumstances. Regardless of what *your* particular situation involves, *all* circumstances can be overcome. You can be free if you want to. Even if you do not want to lead a strict Vanabode lifestyle and enjoy all the benefits it has to offer, you can still use major portions of this guide to better your life.

This book will tell you everything you need to know in order to travel and live comfortably forever from a Vanabode. However, this book is NOT about clever ways to store food in a cooler, or make a fire, or how to charge your computer while on the road: these things *are* covered and are easily accomplished. Nonetheless, the physical gadgets are not the focus of this book. In many cases I will show you how to avoid the problem you seek to solve with that gadget, without buying anything.

The primary focus of this book is to expand your mind; that beautiful, magical, unique to you alone, source of emotion and inspiration. Once you're thinking straight you will be able to address and solve any problem you ever have, whether traveling or not. Once you understand the philosophies that drove me to Vanabode, you will never be the same again. Your mind will expand. Your ideas will be less constrained. Your dreams will no longer seem so unreachable.

Some of the information will make you anxious, uncomfortable, and possibly even angry. Do not fret. Your mind is being stretched to new and better proportions. Truth is replacing the lies you have been told. Truth is eliminating the unhealthy boundaries society has forced you to operate within. Just because I am many rungs behind the writers at the top of the ladder, does not negate the truth I am sharing. Getting mad at truth is a waste of time, allowing it to make you uncomfortable is not.

Vanaboding pares down and eliminates hundreds of expenses and many tasks and pursuits that steal your time; *your life*. Simplification is essential. The fact is you only need these five things in order to have a great life: excellent food, great sleep, good personal hygiene, healthy sex, and protection from the elements. I call these the *Essentials of a Great Life*. The pursuit of anything else will cost you dearly and will rarely adequately reward you.

The truly rich are not those with lots of money, but rather those with *enough time to do what they want to do*. They are *time rich*, which ultimately is everything. Use the techniques and equipment in this book to become truly rich.

When you Vanabode you will have the *time* and money to do things you never had the time to do before. Try fishing, hunting, camping, hiking, stargazing, writing, or composing. Learn to play a portable instrument like the guitar, harmonica or small horn, take a cheap community college course, finish a degree, make jewelry, join a gym, and play a sport like tennis, surf, swim, or snorkel. You can hang out at the library, explore your genealogy, browse the internet, take pictures, look for gold or mine for rocks and minerals, attend a movie, visit an art gallery or museum, walk through a tropical garden, draw or paint a picture, read, study, or build something. You can make crafts and sell them online, pilot a model airplane, helicopter or boat, visit hot springs, ski or take a hot air balloon ride, and ride a bike off-road. These are just examples of activities you can easily do while Vanaboding because they require little money or room in your van.

You will use a simple plain van, properly outfitted with a few gadgets, as your primary source of transportation and lodging. Then you can stealth camp for free, forever, anywhere and everywhere you wish. Use the special tools and cooking strategies to eat healthier and better than you ever have on a micro budget. Outfit the van with a bed so you always have a great night's sleep in comfortable, safe, familiar surroundings. Practice normal personal hygiene without fail and you will always be clean, comfortable and feeling at home in your own skin. Your sex life will improve because you will have eliminated nearly all stress. Finally, your Vanabode will protect you from the elements, in many ways better than a house can.

This book is not just about *traveling* by van. The van can also be used as an emergency preparedness vehicle to get out of the way of a bad snowstorm or hurricane without having to worry about hotels or living in a relative's spare room. It can also be used as a casual getaway vehicle for a 3-6 month trip through the country. Even sitting in your driveway at home, the battery and motor and inverter I recommend can act as a backup generator to provide electricity if the power goes out. The chapters on parking, safety, destinations, privacy, phone strategies, Internet access, handling postal mail, and budgeting, can benefit you even if you do not travel a lot.

One of the greatest benefits to this lifestyle is you will be able to travel at will: go anywhere, for as long as you like, whenever you want. The costs associated with travel in the United States typically run $60 to $200 per day. Vanaboding allows you to have it all: food, lodging and transportation, on $20 a day. The lifestyle saves you money by completely eliminating things you once paid heavily for. Many people actually *increase* the size of their savings account *while traveling* and end up with more money in the bank than they would have had staying home and doing nothing.

Finally this book will show you how to get out of debt so you can reclaim your life. I present resources that outline hundreds of places to work for short periods of time so you can travel at will even if you don't have savings. I also list dozens of methods for running your own business while Vanaboding so you can live boss free forever if you choose.

Vanabode

Vanabode INCLUDES the following to enrich your life through fun affordable travel. I will show you how to have more fun, romance, travel and adventure by happily camping, traveling and living forever on $20 a day. I will show you how and where to apply for thousands of jobs that do not require experience while camping all over the United States in some of the most exciting destinations you have ever imagined. I will show you how to live cheaply off the grid even if you don't want to travel. I will show you how to sleep well, maintain proper personal hygiene with hot showers and toilet strategies, eat delicious exotic meals, all while living a life of adventure; safely, easily, and cheaply. I will show you how to cook hot meals anywhere without electricity, fire or fuel, made from the freshest ingredients, organic fruits, vegetables, meats, artisan breads, and cheeses purchased from thousands of farmers markets. I will show you how to get rid of all your debt and stay debt free forever. I will show foreign travelers and tourists who want to spend 2 months or even 2 years exploring the United States how to do so on cheaply. I will show you how to infuse your life, marriage, and family with the greatest, most romantic memories possible while spending less than a third of what you spend at home doing nothing. I will show you how to happily live a complete and fulfilled life *without* a house. I will show displaced workers, and those struggling financially, how to cut costs and survive with their integrity and dignity intact rather than become homeless. I will show those who don't want a house to keep up with, like young surfers or college students, how to live a fun life without a mortgage payment or the responsibility of a house. I will show RV owners how to happily downsize from their massive motor homes and fifth wheels, all the while saving money and expanding the places they can travel to. I will show short term casual campers, those that wish to keep their 9-5 jobs, and those with large families and young children at home, how to travel and camp simply and cheaply. I will show survivalists or those being stalked, how to disappear, leave their past behind, and become invisible to creditors, government agencies, credit bureaus, and anyone else they wish to limit contact with. I will show those heading for divorce, blaming their spouse rather than their lifestyle for the boredom that is killing them, how to possibly save their marriage. I will show everyone how to get the time and money for a temporary retirement, sabbatical, or extended vacation. I will show you how to get the time off work to write a book, compose music, produce a movie script, or get back on your feet after a divorce or other family tragedy. I will show anyone that wants to run a mobile business like a website, hot dog cart, or consulting company, how to do so with very little overhead. I will show those with a chronic fatal disease how to enjoy life to the fullest before dying.

To Vanabode is to live: *now*. Come with me and you will discover why this revolutionary lifestyle is so unique and sustainable. Unplug your television, shut out the world, curl up in a warm bed behind a closed door and travel to a new destination, forever. I am not talking about a tiny little one-week-a-year trip to a distant place surrounded by tourists where you hope the weather is good and pray you don't get sick and for a few *hours* you can almost forget your tired stress filled life back home. Then you board the plane or ship and head back to your old life; tired, sad and wanting so much more.

NO! I am talking about a method of traveling and living that is so much bigger, so much more sustainable, so much more fun and enriching that once you start you will never live life the same way again. *Vanaboding is about traveling further, easier, cheaper, and for longer periods of time than any other method of travel.* You can see more than you ever thought possible and you can do it on a micro budget, day after day, year after year.

This is not some travel agencies brochure-backed sales pitch designed to profit by taking your precious vacation time and money and then trying to jam a years' worth of fun into five exhausting days. Instead this book contains 19 years' worth of serious road travel experience designed to help you have fun for months or years at a time.

I have lived and traveled this way for many years and I still Vanabode. It works! The crazy thing is many people like myself like it so much we have periodically sold everything and made this our *life!* No mortgage or house to clean and keep up with, no electric bills to pay, no homeowners insurance costs, no homeowners association fees to pay, no water bills to pay, no real estate taxes, no nosy neighbors, no expensive wardrobe for work, no yard maintenance, no schedule to keep, no natural disasters to fear, no ever increasing overwhelming boredom leading to depression, substance abuse, divorce, or even suicide.

Vanabode is built on this principle. You can have right NOW what you are planning on working 30 years to get. Take whatever time you have now and put it to good use. Do something that makes you happy; that helps somebody; that is fun; or that pleases God.

To Vanabode is to reduce life's problems to a bare minimum while maximizing your fun. *You* choose how long to do it. You can make it a 4-day weekend every month or chain together yearlong adventures that could last the rest of your life. Time is the most important requirement for having rich, unforgettable travel experiences; not money. There is a reason Europeans get 6-8 weeks off per year for vacation or as they call it *holiday!* Even if you don't want to travel much you can still use a Vanabode to live comfortably and cheaply in one area.

From the bestseller book, the 4 Hour Workweek, by *Timothy Ferris;* "Being bound to one place will be the new defining feature of the middle class. The New Rich are defined by a more elusive power than simple cash - unrestricted mobility." If this is not the essence of the Vanabode, I don't know what is.

Vanabode candidates include: anyone who is so bored with their lifestyle that they feel like they are barely living, those trapped by household expenses so great that they never get ahead and rarely get to do anything fun, families with children who want to camp cheaply, retirees, RV owners downsizing from large motor homes, displaced workers, sabbatical seekers, college students, outdoor enthusiasts, artists, musicians, foreign tourists, survivalists, those wanting to disappear, the chronically ill, and people moving and wanting to investigate new areas cheaply without the commitment of an expensive purchase or lease.

Vanabode by definition: *to happily abide in a four wheeled box shaped vehicle providing transportation and housing.* This is not the *only* way to travel or live a free life on the road. But it is absolutely the best way to travel and live affordably because it is safer, cheaper, faster, more sustainable, and easier than every other method.

When Vanaboding you will sleep in your own bed just like you do at your house. You can have a hot shower or bath every day. You can afford to eat out at new and exciting restaurants every day because you won't be blowing money on much else. You can cook hot meals while on the road, made from the freshest ingredients, organic fruits, vegetables, and artisan breads, meats and cheeses, from local produce stands around the country.

Many elements make up a great travel day including landscapes, terrain, wild life, interesting characters, structures, sounds, smells, and colors. The warm embracing sunshine reflecting off a shear canyon wall, the eerie silence and wet weight of an early morning fog, the icy cool mist drifting up from a waterfall, the rapidly changing atmospheric pressure of a cave two miles underground, the light quality of a cloudless sky, the sound of your partners laughter when they are completely happy, the crisp coolness of your clean shady bed on a hot day: you can have all this and more when Vanaboding.

Where Do We Live?

Some laugh at the thought of *living in a van*. But you don't really *live* in any one place regardless of your lifestyle. For example: take the typical apartment dweller in a larger U.S. city. They are at their job for at least 9 hours a day with a lunch break, spend about 2 hours a day traveling to and from work, sleep 8 hours a day, use the bathroom and shower about 1 hour a day, **leaving only 4 hours a day** for the hundreds of tasks that make up life: chores, shopping for groceries, going to the doctors, yard work, meal preparation, getting the car serviced, etc. When asked where they live they say *"I live in an apartment at 123 Smith Street"* Ha! What a joke! They barely spend an average of 4 waking hours of disposable time a day in that apartment and when they do they are just sitting there exhausted in front of the television or on the toilet or doing dishes or cleaning. I hardly call that *living at 123 Smith Street!*

So when you Vanabode you aren't really *living in a van*. What you are doing is traveling, camping, sleeping and recuperating from all the fun you have been having **all day** because you had the time and money to do so. This is the real key to this lifestyle. It frees up your most precious resource, your time, as well as your money, so you can do the things you really want to do. So you can really *live.*

Do you have a terribly misconstrued idea of where you *live?* We don't live in houses, condos, apartment buildings, boats, tents, or any other kind of structure. *We live in our bodies!* That's right. We are created beings. You can understand how this plays out by understanding this simple fact: We *are* a spirit, we *have* a mind, and we *live* in a body. The lifestyle that I am advocating is far superior to that of trading your body (your real home) in 30 years of toil to a boss you dislike, in a job you hate, just so you can have enough money to buy a house to sleep in. A house that you will leave to others that have not worked for it, when you die.

Many Americans that get caught up in the lie called the *American Dream* do exactly this: they work to buy then die. This is also known as the *deferred life plan*; where you attend school and work for the first 40 years of your adult life so you can *live* when you retire at age 60 or later. Many that follow this plan end up with broken marriages, alienated children, crushed dreams, boredom, obesity, poor health, and a house to sleep away the pain in and further propagate the nightmare. Why does this happen? Because we are taught that we cannot *live* unless we have a *house* to do it in. Nonsense! Not everyone needs a house. Even those who want a house now, will at many times in their life wish they did not have it, and could instead do something else with their life.

Is Vanaboding weird? Yes, maybe it is in a quirky alternative lifestyle kind of way: but not nearly as weird as you might think. Hundreds of millions of people all over the world live in substandard housing that is much more dangerous and much less comfortable than my specially outfitted van. Some use shack huts that literally fall down every year. Some sleep in their cars. Many board up 10 to 12 per house in upscale cities like San Francisco giving up all sense of privacy because the rents are so high. Our soldiers in uniform live for years in tents in foreign lands. The entire worlds homeless billions live unprotected debilitating lives in the most inhumane of places. Multitudes live aboard ramshackle boats tied by the thousands one to the next in a floating city of Asian humanity. Hundreds of thousands of cruise boat employees sleep in tiny bunks in tiny 5 x 10 foot windowless floating cabins for 9 months straight before getting extended leave to go ashore. Mr. Nasseri lived in the lounge of a famous Paris airport for over 10 years. Since 2000, Daniel Suelo has happily lived in a cave outside Moab.

So mainstream America, compared to all this, is Vanaboding really all that weird? Not really. I'll take the Vanabode lifestyle or some close version of it over these choices any day.

This brings us to the millions who live in fancy houses and condos in developed nations like the United States. We have built great houses to choose from, but; and here's the key, we don't own them, nor do we have the wherewithal to maintain them without working until we are nearly dead, trapped in debt, despair and fatigue. Does it make sense to be unable to do anything more than work to pay off our mortgages? Would you rather have a sweet debt free lifestyle traveling and having fun all week than a boredom filled house supported by endless years of work? Maybe not.

I have seen the spirits of many of my friends and even my own, quickly shrivel up once the home maintenance and mortgage paying process kicks in. It looks like they are actually living and dying without hope like my ancestors the American Indians did towards the end.

The most successful early Native American Indians like the Comanche, Apache, and Cheyenne practiced a transient mobile lifestyle via horseback not unlike the modern day *snow bird* or Vanaboder. That is, they lived so they could travel at will, to anywhere that was more pleasant than where they currently were. I was told I am descended from French and American Indian ancestry. Maybe another reason why I like this life so much.

These early relatives of mine had other peculiar perspectives on life that intuitively made their mobile life more agreeable. For example John Fire Lame Deer is generally credited with sharing this information, but I paraphrase as the text comes in various versions. *"Before whites came the Indians had no criminals because they had no jails. You can't have a criminal without a jail. They didn't have locks and keys, so they had no thieves. If anybody was poor and needed a horse or blanket, someone owning an extra horse or blanket gave it to him. They didn't have money, so a man's worth couldn't be measured by it. They did not have any written laws, which meant no attorneys or politicians, so they couldn't cheat."* Many Indians lived a simple life unencumbered by much of the stress and life sucking responsibilities embraced as normal by present day Americans.

In the recent past white Australians tried to keep the Aborigines as cheap labor. They used the term *walkabout* to describe one of the methods the Aborigines used to escape the mindless work. "That lazy one just up and left his job and went walkabout." The native Aborigines, so bored and oppressed by the white man's 7-5 grind, would literally just stop working, put down their tools right in the middle of the day, and without warning or notice, simply walk away. To keep from going stir crazy at the white man's manual labor jobs, they go on walkabout, into the wilderness and are not seen again for months. Sometimes they are not seen again for a year or more.

This is the power behind being able to *walk away* or in my case Vanabode. Does your lifestyle afford you this? Can you travel at will, or do you need permission first? Are you a free man or woman? You were made to be. You can be.

To Vanabode is to be on an adventure without much real sacrifice. You can live a fun life filled with excellent food, laughter, big romantic adventures, healthy sex, protection from the elements, and a good night's sleep. You can have this at very little cost. The best thing is it is sustainable: you can happily, safely and affordably Vanabode for many years or even for the rest of your life. What else do you need?

Vanabode Versus Other Living Strategies

Vanabode versus air car hotel travel - Vanaboding is better than air and car travel combined with hotel stays. With hotels you have to make, pay for and keep reservations. You have to coordinate check in and check out times and wrap everything you do throughout your trip around these times. You cannot come and go as you wish. You are limited in what you can carry with you. You give up your freedom. You often hear, smell and otherwise come in contact with people in adjacent rooms: people you do not know or want to know. You do not get to sleep in your own bed. I do not want to sleep in a bed that had who knows who in it, doing who knows what, two hours prior to my arrival. Do you?

I also prefer a certain mattress density, linens, and pillows. So, while in my van, I get the best possible sleep, whereas in a hotel I rarely do, regardless of how fancy it is. Hotel rooms are expensive. I would rather spend my money on extraordinary meals, movies, parks, shows, clubs, museums, zoos, botanical gardens, adventure and having fun! Besides, did you ever think about what you are really paying for when you stay in a hotel room? You spend 80% of the time you are actually in the room *asleep*.

Summary: Air, car and hotel travel is very expensive, has complicated and very limiting time constraints, is nearly always less comfortable than sleeping in your own bed, and subjects you to close contact with strangers. On the other hand if you Vanabode you will have the opportunity to travel where you want, when you want, cheaply, comfortably, and without contact with anyone, if you so choose.

Vanabode versus large motor homes, RV's or travel trailers - Vanaboding is better than typical recreational vehicle travel for many reasons. I know because I traveled the country for years and lived full time in both a Class C and a Class A motorhome (http://www.rvforsaleguide.com/fulltime-rv.htm) before discovering this far superior and much simpler lifestyle. Vanaboding is *much* cheaper. The initial rental or purchase of the van costs much less than the initial rental or purchase of a full sized RV. The van depreciates much less than the larger specialized RV's. The van costs nothing to sleep in, whereas throughout the country you will pay $16 to $120 a night to park and hook up your motorhome. My van gets 15-18 miles per gallon whereas most big motorhome or truck trailer combinations average 5-9 miles per gallon.

I can travel at highway road speeds of up to 80 miles per hour if I want to get somewhere fast. If you travel that fast in a motorhome or travel trailer you risk a serious accident. Vans outfitted like mine have no permanent plumbing and therefore are classified as a personal passenger vehicle. Homeowners associations and city governments all over the country have enacted laws prohibiting RV's from parking anywhere outside a paid campground (this is how they tax you even if you choose to not own a house). The Vanabode is *not* classified as an RV. This means you can use the Vanabode as your personal transportation and keep it at your house. You can also use cheap passenger car insurance rather than specialized more expensive RV insurance. Ultimately this means you can legally park for free in millions of places that have enforceable ordinances *against* RV parking.

Vans are super easy to drive, steer, park, and maneuver off road. However, driving an oversized RV will make you very tired and will stress you out in traffic. You can rarely take a large recreational vehicle off road to the more interesting, secluded places that we go. Even the national parks like Yellowstone, Glacier and Zion have heavy restrictions on large vehicles, whereas you can go everywhere in the van. There are hundreds of areas in California and big cities like Las Vegas, San Francisco and New York City that are virtually impossible to explore with a large motorhome.

If I am going to turtle over thousands of miles, it makes sense to do so with the smallest possible shell. Thus the van becomes a superior choice to the monstrous motorhome.

Summary: Large RV's can be more comfortable than a van but you have to pay so much more in terms of upfront money, fuel costs, and camping costs that they are not worth it if you are on budget. With typical RV's and trailers you are usually limited to staying in campgrounds which restricts what you can see and do, and subjects you to crowded, noisy conditions. Vanaboding is *much* cheaper. Vans are easier to drive enabling you to see virtually everything in this country without restriction; from wild off road primitive wilderness camping to fine museums and art galleries.

Vanabode versus living in a house - There are those who for one reason or another just can't, at some time in their life, *happily* reside in a house or apartment. Sometimes it's the costs of keeping up a residence that ruins it for them: like paying rent, utility bills, mortgage payments, taxes, HOA fees, and maintenance. Sometimes its other things that take the fun out of staying put, like sheer boredom, bad noisy neighbors, or climate changes that effect allergies and health.

The sheer logistics of Vanaboding are just better than housing up someplace. For instance, when you want to disappear because you might be running from obnoxious people, debt, bad memories, or stalkers, it is easy to get away and remain anonymous when you don't have to sign a lease somewhere or have your credit run. Stay in your van. Have fun. Be invisible. The must have Privacy Resource (http://www.vanabode.com/camp/hide-your-money-privacy.htm) will explain all this. The **Disappear** chapter in this book covers this in more detail as well.

Sometimes people need a change and they don't want to be tied down to one place. Besides, home ownership is a huge commitment and responsibility. Poker players polishing their skills at various casinos throughout the US don't want to spend their bankrolls on rent. People on sabbatical needing fresh air to think and relax and get their life back in order don't want to be stuck in the middle of a noisy Detroit or a polluted Los Angeles or any inner city for that matter. Those with a chronic illness who need to get out and live as much as they can before it's over, will find the Vanabode lifestyle ideal, and home ownership a drag. In nearly every conceivable situation having the ability to be mobile trumps living out of a house.

Henry David Thoreau said in his great book *Walden* "I used to see a large box by the railroad, six feet long by three wide, in which the laborers locked up their tools at night; and it suggested to me that every man who was hard pushed might get such a one for a dollar, and, having bored a few auger holes in it, to admit the air at least, get into it when it rained and at night, and hook down the lid, and so have freedom in his love, and in his soul be free. This did not appear the worst, nor by any means a despicable alternative. You could sit up as late as you pleased, and, whenever you got up, go abroad without any landlord or house-lord dogging you for rent. Many a man is harassed to death to pay the rent of a larger and more luxurious box who would not have frozen to death in such a box as this."

Now this is beautiful writing and embraceable philosophy. He reduces complicated expensive home ownership, to instead paying a dollar for a large toolbox to sleep in; without landlord; without rent. Simple. Doable. Empowering. He goes on to establish the truth that the poor man can own his own shelter *because it costs so little* (cue Vanabode) while the civilized high society man cannot afford his house because his greed and ego require he have one that is too big, too fancy, and too expensive. Because he is not easily pleased he chooses to overpay by getting a 30 year mortgage or overpay by renting, *forever*. Remember, the true cost of something is not realized in dollars, but rather by how much of your time (your life) must be exchanged *for* the dollars to acquire that something.

The Homestead Act written back in the mid 1800's GAVE 160 acres to anyone who would live on the land for FREE! Compare that to today's pathetic options. Have you seen the ridiculous commercials with some young people joyfully hugging each other? Why? Well they just got themselves a 30-year prison sentence called a mortgage on a *crappy drywall box to sleep in sitting on a tiny lot!* Do you see how far we have fallen in just 150 years?

Your life will be immeasurably improved when you spend more time outside, even if you don't consider yourself a rugged outdoors person. I always laugh at the fools on the big million dollar house shows, because the first thing they do with all that money is try to bring the *outdoors in*. They spend half their budget on location: mountaintop, beachfront, river view, etc. Then they put massive floor to ceiling windows so they can see everything *out* there, they put huge sliding glass doors leading *out* to the gardens, swimming pools, and trees. Then they have to protect, insure, repair, maintain, and pay hundreds of thousands of dollars in taxes, utility bills, insurance premiums, and maintenance every year. Why do they do all this? To SEE outside.

You can have all that right now without the million dollar budget or the running expenses that commence the second you buy a building. How can you get everything the rich have without paying for it? Drive your Vanabode where you like the view. Get out. Look. Problem solved. Remember they don't really seek bigger houses. They seek bigger views, bigger gardens, bigger unspoiled wilderness and bigger experiences to go with them. Vanabode and you naturally have all that by default.

When people first here of trouble the mobile traveler has options those holed up in a house do not. With your Vanabode you can easily and instantly escape that coming tornado, hurricane, social unrest, forest fire, flood, or nasty neighbor. You can't do that with a house. What do the homeowners do to counteract the inevitable disasters that will come upon their house? They spend thousands and thousands of dollars year after year for insurance.

Purchasing an expensive dwelling via a soul crushing 30-year mortgage is just plain stupid when you can own your life *now* by purchasing a smaller dwelling. For example, you can purchase a Vanabode that will last for 20 years; for the cost of owning a house for just *one* year.

I am not entirely against home ownership, but for those that cannot enjoy their life because they are trying to buy more house than they need, I suggest alternatives. Buy a small cheap house that you can pay off in less than 5 years; one that allows you lots of time to play. If you must purchase a house make sure that it does not cage you, but *serves* you. If your house keeps you from doing the things you want to do, then you're in prison, under *house* arrest.

One of the smartest things I have seen done by travelers who own a house is renting it out instead of living in it. Example: you are working 50 hours a week to maintain your house and local life, taking a one week vacation once a year. You want more time for yourself. So you trade your car for a Vanabode, quit your job, rent out your house, and travel the rest of your life on the rental income.

Summary: The time, money and effort spent owning and living in a house is so great that many people become overwhelmed. They are overcome with boredom and stop enjoying life altogether. They travel very little. They don't have fun and consequently their love life becomes stagnant. In debt, tied to their jobs, most of their years disappear. On the other hand if you Vanabode you can live free, cheap and travel everywhere. You can avoid debt and huge time commitments while *Prioritizing Your Pleasure* (more on this later).

Vanabode versus backpacking - Backpacking may be the cheapest means of travel in terms of hard cash expenditures, but it comes at a heavy real life cost. Backpackers give up nearly all their privacy and personal safety. They are often perceived as homeless and then referred to as bums. They frequently have nowhere to bathe. They are exposed to people, animals, and the weather every time they sleep, urinate, defecate, or even change clothes.

Backpackers cannot easily keep in touch via cell phone or Internet unless they are city bound, because the only practical reliable ways to charge the batteries is purchasing expensive specialized finicky solar energy type equipment, which they then have to protect from theft. Backpackers also move at a painfully slow pace.

Many backpackers think that they get to see more of nature than van campers. This is not true. Backpackers have to stay near food and water to survive. They cannot carry more than 4 days' worth of food and water in a backpack so they often head into town or to some little store to buy more. By contrast, my wife and I happily star gaze, hike, swim, and play from our Vanabode in very remote areas with a months' worth of food and water stored safely under our bed.

As a backpacker you have to be in very good shape to enjoy sleeping on the hard ground, out in the weather, after tromping miles over rough terrain in the sun, rain, cold and wind. While on a Vanabode trip though, your nice warm, dry, comfortable bed is waiting for you upon returning from that hike along with clean clothes, a toilet, water to bathe off with, and seriously good fresh food.

Backpacking also severely limits the activities you get to enjoy. When Vanaboding I go to all the good restaurants, clubs, museums, art galleries, public libraries, botanical gardens, and more, that a city or geographical area has to offer; while the stinky unshaven backpack toter is told *"sorry sir but we have a dress code"* or *"sir, no backpacks are allowed at this event for the safety of others."*

Summary: The severe limitations involved with backpacking make this nothing more than a short temporary excursion choice for all but the most hardened and adventurous. However, Vanaboding enables you to do nearly every single thing the backpacker does *plus* hundreds of things the backpacker cannot do. Vanaboding is much safer than backpacking especially for the single person. Vanaboding is faster, easier, healthier and more practical long term.

Vanabode versus houseboats, motor yachts, powerboats, and sailboats - Life on the water poses many challenging and difficult situations for which the average person has no answer. Severe weather is a constant headache threatening both life and bankroll. Boats are extremely expensive to purchase initially. Maintenance costs are the highest of any form of living. Living on the water requires the highest level of personal time to manage as well.

The confined small spaces of a boat can wreak havoc with claustrophobia on some people, and make even the closest pair want to strangle each other. Seasickness can be hard to overcome. Daily vomiting is common. Boredom is a constant issue with longer voyages.

One possible exception to most of these issues, is the live aboard houseboat in protected inland waters like the Florida Intracoastal Waterway or Lake Powell, Utah. In these places you could theoretically stay forever for free. As long as you can overcome boredom through the use of a solar powered satellite Internet and cable TV connection or by fishing and snorkeling all day, you might be okay.

Summary: Only the most seaworthy and adventurous people will find live aboard boating of interest due to the severe destination limitations, heavy doses of danger, and major expenses involved in this extraordinary lifestyle. Vanaboding is safer, easier, and cheaper, and offers more travel location options. Vanaboders can still rent a boat or take a two week long cruise if they want. This alleviates long term financial commitments too.

Vanabode versus car camping is simply no contest. With car camping you are constantly cramped, have nowhere to use the bathroom, have little to no privacy, cannot sleep flat, and have severe storage limitations. Off road trips are more difficult or impossible since cars do not typically have enough ground clearance. You cannot sleep wherever you want as people can look right in at you. The seats are made to form fit the seated upright person not someone lying flat. Car campers may have a tiny advantage up front over the van buyer because the car might cost less up front and cost less to fuel. But that is not much.

Summary: Anyone who takes more than a week or two and car camps rather than Vanaboding is making a mistake. Vanaboding is better in every way possible. Before going on your journey trade your car for a van like the one I recommend.

Vanabode versus being homeless - With the economy so bad many thousands of people are without a residence to call *home.* Many people cannot afford to rent or buy a house. Many have poor credit. Some are not mentally prepared to manage a household. These people are congregating by the thousands in homeless shelters, day shelters, food banks, under bridges, on the streets and alleys, and in the woods and public parks.

All over the country, in the last few years, police have moved in on the tent cities of the homeless, one by one, from Maine to Key West, from Seattle to San Diego, in night time raids, taking everything the homeless have. A volunteer told about the smash and grab dispersion of a tent city, "The *city* will not tolerate a *tent city."* These people living in tents cannot be taxed, so they are harassed, chased, and prodded like cattle from one pasture to the next by city governments and law enforcement.

If you are a homeless American you might as well be a fugitive. These folks are treated worse than illegal aliens sometimes. They face laws that prevent them from doing normal human duties. They are not supposed to be seen. They are not supposed to ruin public places with their waste. They are supposed to hide their exhausted bodies. *Joe public,* as presented by local government bodies and laws, does not want to see their clothes, their bedding, or their unshaven faces. They are made to feel like it would just be better for everybody else if they just died (often presented as "go away" or "disappear.")

While the laws vary from city to city, one of the harshest was enacted in Sarasota, Florida back in 2005. That law made it illegal to "engage in digging or earth-breaking activities" which means it is an arrestable offense to dig a small hole to urinate or defecate in. You break the law if you make a fire to cook with or to stay warm with. You are actually not even allowed to be asleep and "when awakened, state that you have no other place to live." In other words they are trying to make it illegal to be homeless or live outdoors for any reason. To the original inhabitants of this awesome land this would have been unfathomable. I find it unforgiveable. It will certainly take a revolution in this country to stop the wealthy from imposing on people's simple existence and unalienable rights.

Until then I propose you drive around the problem altogether. The answer to all this is to Vanabode where you can safely and comfortably live on $20 a day and not be a burden or nuisance to anyone. If you stay in one area some people can do it for $10 a day. Those that have bought my book are living large compared to how they once lived in shared crowded overpriced rooms in big expensive cities like San Francisco and New York City. Many work $12 an hour jobs as bread makers, fast food attendants, and other service jobs. Before Vanaboding they spent so much of their income on housing they became destitute. Now though, hundreds have a comfortable place to call home. Now their dignity is restored and they are clean, safe, and presentable while saving money.

In 2013 National Public Radio reported that there were at least 45 million homeless refugees currently in the world. They are alive, living, breathing, eating, and sleeping. They are doing so without houses. They may not be comfortable, but they are nevertheless, alive. I am *not* telling you to live in a cave, or to live in a shack in a Brazilian favela, or to live as a refugee. I *am* telling you that there are multitudes of people from all walks of life, of all nationalities, of all ages, living and sleeping in much worse conditions than that of a comfortable, safe, affordable Vanabode.

Summary: practicing homelessness is not usually a person's first choice. It is difficult, dangerous, demeaning, and even illegal in some places. Vanaboding is safer, easier, healthier, and much better on your self-esteem.

Vanabode presents the best exit strategy. When you Vanabode you have one very big advantage over most every other style of living. You have a low commitment level and very little risk. Everything you purchase to Vanabode with, from the van itself to the bed and all the small gear, can still be used to lead a more typical life later, if you find you don't like it. You don't buy anything to Vanabode that cannot be incorporated easily into other lifestyles or sold for what you paid for it, if you want to quit. On the other hand, if you purchase a large motorhome for $180,000 or a get a $300,000 mortgage on a house, you are committed. You cannot easily change your mind and move on. You are now very upside down financially. You must stay with it for many years just to break even, and be able to sell out and move on. Boats are even worse in this regard.

We Never Own Anything

If you do not get anything else from this book; get this. It is the most important principle I have every introduced. *We never own anything!* There is no such thing as *owning* something! You never, ever, own anything! Everything is borrowed from someone else, is on loan from the Earth, and ultimately borrowed from God. People everywhere misunderstand this truth. They are the primary reason behind the current global economic failure. Greed driven ownership hungry people, including myself, recently invested in the housing and stock markets, and are now suffering because they failed to understand this simple fact!

What people are seeking, when they seek the ownership of something; is *control.* When they buy a house they are not trying to experience sweaty tiring yard work, the paying of huge mortgages, electric bills, repairs, insurance, water bills, trash handling, sewage, real estate taxes, mortgage interest, theft, or worrying about natural disasters like floods, hurricanes and fire. NO! They are only trying to gain *control* by owning the box they sleep in! They want to be able to tell others "I *own* that house. I can do anything I want with it. You can't take it away from me."

But this is a *lie!* It's all a lie. Stop paying your mortgage payment or insurance premium and see if you own that house then. Stop paying your taxes, even after you have paid the mortgage off, and see who owns your house. Watch as it burns or is swept away in a flood or blown apart in a hurricane and see what you own. When you lay on your deathbed do you really think it will matter if you have your silly little signature on some deed in a drawer somewhere? No! Somebody else is right there bedside, taking the house you thought you *owned.*

When you die, others who did not work for it, will quickly take everything you *thought* you owned. Your body is even on loan to you for a few years, then taken back to the dust from which it came. This fact is no mystery. God pointed this out many years ago. "*What doth it profit a man if he gains the whole world, but loses his own soul?*" Don't just read the question. *Answer it.*

In 2009 the average household net worth for the top **1%** was widely reported as nearly *14 million dollars*, while the average household net worth for **the bottom 47% was ZERO.** That means almost HALF of America doesn't *own* any more than it *owes!* So what is everybody running around working 40 to 60 hours a week for; leaving no time for themselves? What are *you* working for? Is what you will achieve what you are seeking? Do you practice a gross kind of lazy thinking that keeps you so busy you cannot be bothered to stop and think hard, and ask, *"Could I be doing something better with my short life?"*

Psalm 39:6 New Living Translation sums this up: "*We are merely moving shadows, and all our busy rushing ends in nothing. We heap up wealth, not knowing who will spend it.*"

I have friends that bought a house before they were completely ready because they couldn't save fast enough to keep up with the rising prices. They figured even with the house as overpriced as it was; if they didn't buy now they would never be able to buy a house. They took out a huge mortgage. The market crashed. They lost all the money they paid as a down payment. They lost all the money they spent on modifications, repairs, maintenance, insurance, taxes, and closing costs. They lost 12 years' worth of savings. Then they lost the house. Then they lost their good credit.

Guess what? I lost two properties exactly the same way, a gorgeous condo located just one half mile from the Las Vegas strip and a brand new custom 2,000 square foot house in the beautiful desert. When my websites made a little extra money I was told by my financial advisors to "invest in real estate, it is safer than stocks and will never go down". Seriously, this is exactly what they told me. I lost over $90,000 over the course of 3 years during the housing bust because I tried to *own* (control) more than I needed.

People are renting huge storage places to stockpile the junk that they bought, but have no room for, in their 5,000 square foot house. That *stuff* that they don't need or use came from the Earth. The raw materials to make that stuff were stolen and mined from the Earth, assembled with slave labor, processed using irreplaceable fossil fuels, transported half way around the world using pollution spewing ships and trucks, sold, and then stored. It makes me want to vomit.

The incredible entrepreneur Wang Chuan-Fu grew up in extreme poverty but now owns a company that employs hundreds of thousands of people. The train ride to school every day took him past the tourist destination Yellow Mountain. He has never visited it. "I didn't go then because I had no money," he says. "I don't go now because I have no time." Even the best of the best are getting it wrong. He spent all his early years in school to learn how to run a business and now spends all his later years managing the great money making monster that *he thinks he owns.*

I paraphrase *Ecclesiastes*, "We spend years in school, followed by years of work, so that we can accumulate possessions, only to see death snatch them away and give them to others whose attitudes and actions we do not agree with, and to those we cannot control."

Stop worrying about what you think you own, what you think others own, and what you think you should be trying to own, in order to have a fulfilled life. Stop trying to *buy* a fun life. Live the one you have been given. You are free right? You don't need a house, or two, or three, and you don't need more stuff.

People die and others take their place, and take their houses, and take their possessions. You do not know how much time you have. You cannot add to the time you have. You cannot replace your time. Spend it wisely. *Spend time often* on love and memorable activities, remembering always that you do not; now, nor will you ever, *own* anything. Why not live the 10-20 years of retirement (you think you will have later) *now?*

The love of money is the desire to *control things.* You don't lovingly caress a handful of $100 dollar bills because they are pretty or nice to the touch. Rather you get excited because you can control portions of your life with that wad of cash. When everyone else is eating burgers and fries, you can choose to eat steak and lobster. When everyone else is renting a one-bedroom apartment in a crowded building, you can purchase a mansion on the lake.

So if you love money, what you have just read is the good news. *That's all the good news there is.* "Well isn't that enough?" you ask. "I like being in control. I like doing what I want, when I want. The power to control the people, objects and elements around me with my money must be life's greatest pleasure right?" **Wrong.** Here's why.

1) We never own anything as explained in this chapter. This is a core precept that will save you hundreds of thousands of dollars and countless hours of heartache over the course of your life if you make it part of your thinking. Understanding this will put you far ahead of your peers and serve to give you a sense of peace unobtainable without it.

2) You control nothing once dead. Every dollar you have with you when you die represents missed opportunities, and wasted hours and years of life that you will never get

back. Example: a man works 50 years in a hated factory job, saving $1,000 a year so at age 70 he retires with $50,000 plus interest. Then he dies a year later. Each of the 50 years of working the job he hated, served to do nothing more than feed, clothe and house him, so he could continue working the next year. The 50,000 in savings that he thought he was really working *for* was never his. His *time* was the only thing that was really his. And this most precious gift was gone, traded for money in the bank that he never got the chance to use.

3) Money is an illusion. Ask any poor person what they want more of and they usually answer "money". Ask any rich person the same question and they *never* answer "money". They usually mumble this pitiful reply, "I wish I had more *time:* time with friends; time with family; free time away from business; more time to play. Instead I was too busy." Money is not real. It is just numbered sheets of paper used so we don't have to murder each other to get a loaf of bread.

Every physical pleasure incurs an equal penalty when abused. Smoke too much; get lung cancer. Sleep around; contract HIV. Eat too much; get fat. Practicing a greedy lifestyle, trying to own and control too much of the space and objects around you, also brings about a penalty. You cannot have more than you are due. God: through the agents of nature, gravity, depreciation, aging, disease, thieves, pestilence, and finally death, sees to it that none gets more than they deserve. Everybody pays up at some point. Thievery takes place where those that have more than they need come in contact with those that do not have enough.

Now we arrive at my final point in this regard. *If you do not buy your life back with your money you have wasted all the resources you used to get the money.* Your money is worthless if you do not buy back your time with it. If you have $200,000 saved and you are still working 50 hours a week to pay all the bills on your high profile life you are making a HUGE mistake. Sell the expensive car. Sell the expensive house. Downsize to the smallest cheapest vehicle and buy or rent the smallest cheapest house or apartment you can find. Then you can quit your job, and take the $100,000 or more you got from selling your high maintenance stuff and downsizing, and spend it doing what you really wanted to do with your life all along. If you are not so rich employ the Vanabode strategies in this book to break free from debt and work slavery. Either way *buy your life back.*

I am not preaching *at* you. I am writing about this subject because I too have blundered thus. I have spent considerable portions of my time and life in the fruitless pursuit of more money, control, and power. I have put the important things in life second. I have invested in America's lies and paid the consequences for it. I have learned these lessons late, between the ages of 40 and 44; but better now than never.

So, live your life possessing and controlling as little as possible. You will not be disappointed. Minute by minute you will feel the freedom from living such an unencumbered life. Do not let wealth destroy your poverty. To the workaholic I ask, "You are only 30 years old and already you labor towards your burial?" Instead embrace simplicity and all the joys that come with your newfound treasure; your time.

Simplify

To simplify means to minimize hassles and stress by reducing unpleasant experiences and time stealing chores. You do this through proper planning, flexibility and by expanding your mind. Stop watching commercials. Start thinking. Ask yourself what is worth the time and money and energy to bring within your control. You have to make choices in life. When traveling, it is even more important to realize what is important and what is not. Simplicity is rarely more costly or problematic than complicated attempts to solve problems that are best just avoided. *"If you need it, but you don't have it; then you may not need it."*

Your approach to getting what you want may be flawed. In fact, you probably don't really even know what you want or what you really need. Consumers are tricked all the time to buy stuff they are told will do it for them, but which in fact does little to satisfy. You may already have all the resources needed to begin a 6 month Vanabode trip. From there you can transition into full time forever travel. The money for this is stored in stuff you bought, stuff you don't need, stuff you rarely use, and stuff you shouldn't own.

Often you can have what you want *without* buying it. For example; you want to watch television tonight so you decide you need to *buy* a television. That means you have to have a house to put it in, then pay an electric bill, and pay a cable bill, and you have to worry about theft, pay for repairs and maintenance, pay the initial cost, and pay to have it replaced when it dies. If you approach this problem using traditional American consumerist thinking, then all these worries are necessary because you *had* to have them in order to have a television to watch. Right? WRONG!

What you actually wanted was to *watch* TV not *own* one. So skip all the nonsense I have outlined above and get straight to having what you want. While traveling you can see a movie at a theatre, rent a DVD and watch it on your computer in the van, stop at a friend's house for some tube time, or simply hit any number of thousands of pubs, bars, and clubs all over the country. Many have anywhere from 5 to 30 televisions waiting for you, playing all sorts of programs. Free. No house needed. No bills to pay. No maintenance, cost, or theft to worry about.

Consider a lifestyle different from your typical consume all you can, wasteful, I am filthy rich and I can buy anything I want, approach to life. That is what has destroyed our economy, wrecked our housing market and negatively impacted every country in the world. Greed. Stupidity. Everyone driving their Mercedes Benz sedans straight off the cliff. Here it is in a nutshell. Take out a pen and write down these words. Think about them. Enact them. *Just because I think I have a need, want, or desire, does not mean the best solution is to buy something.*

The *big* problems in life can't be solved with money anyway, so what makes us think the medium problems can? Can you cure your child's cancer with your million dollars? Can you pay to put your broken marriage back together? Can you write a check and ensure God will grant you Heaven instead of Hell? Can you pay to get your child off drugs? No, you can't; and neither can I.

The other issues that so many of us have been told can be solved by buying more stuff, cannot be solved this way either. You will not be happy *just* because you buy a house. In fact you will probably feel ripped off, tired and trapped at some point. You will not be happy just because you have three fancy cars. They get old, depreciate, scratched, and break down like everything else. The boat, the RV, the horse, the motorcycle, the 4-wheeler, the Jet Ski, and the other toys won't make you happy either. Why? Because by the time you have paid for them, paid to ensure them, paid to protect them, paid to store them, paid to maintain them, and paid to actually use them, you will have worked so long and hard you won't have the *energy or time* to actually use them. You won't have new places to take them because you are trapped in one place unable to leave. You won't have the pleasure you were told you would have when you bought them. You will pay for them and when they are done depreciating you will sell them for one tenth what you paid for them.

We have it all wrong. When you bought the house you just wanted a safe place to bathe, eat and sleep. Instead you got a prison with a 30-year sentence or *mortgage* as the bankers call it. When you bought the cool cars, you thought they would impress your mate, and keep your marriage together. In reality your mate just wanted *time with you*, not a new car with you off working even more hours to pay for it. When you bought the boat you thought it would bring your family together and give you the ability to go fishing. Wrong. Between your jobs, keeping up the house to store the boat at, the maintenance on the boat, and the extra hours you have to work to pay for it all, the joy of owning it has evaporated. What you wanted was to *go fishing and have fun*, not *own* a boat. Now you have another headache filled portion of your life sucked dry by loose ends, fatigue and boat payments.

When Vanaboding with your partner you can have a completely fulfilled life unencumbered by debt, boredom or strife. You can be free. It will take changing your mind about things, addressing problems intelligently instead of by habit, and modifying your behavior. In the end you get what you really want. A simple, wonderful, fun filled, nearly hassle free life. You can do it. You can do it *your way* by using the principles in this book to address your own needs and desires, to add fun to your life, and to have some adventure.

Simplify by *backing up;* your thought process that is. For example, when considering the purchase of new stove ask yourself "why do I need a new stove?" Your initial answer will be "it will enable me to cook better meals, my husband will enjoy that, so it will bring us closer together." In reality if you have not taken the time to become a good cook because you work too much, then a new stove will do nothing for meal quality. The reality is, your husband will probably not eat any better or be any happier with the new stove. You probably won't either. Why? Because your cooking has not changed. You both are still tired when you get home from work. You are still eating the same food on the same table in the same dining room with the same person.

In fact ask him, "Honey, would you rather buy me this new $900 oven, then schedule the delivery, then get rid of the old one, so I can bake a turkey *6 months from now* for Thanksgiving and have the in-laws over to eat: OR would you rather I make your favorite sandwich, buy some special drinks, and go have lunch under that big shade tree in the park *right now*?" The difference is clear.

What you were *really* wanting with the new oven was a way to spend more time with your mate eating a great meal in a romantic place. Well that can be achieved *without* the expensive new stove and it can be achieved *now*. For example in the **Food** chapter I show you how to cook *on the road* in exciting romantic places using many different methods, one of them completely free. That's right, you can prepare hot nourishing meals for free, without electricity, fire, smoke, wood, or fuel of any kind.

Have you ever run your vacuum cleaner back and forth, first from the right then from the left, forced zigzagging, crisscrossing, overlapping, over and over, because dammit; *I paid a lot of money for this vacuum and I took the time to drag it out, and plug it in, and roll it over here. I will NOT simply bend over and pick up that little piece of paper on the floor; even if it would only take me half a second.* To do that would be to face the fact that this tool, this vacuum, was not necessary to make you happy. It was not a necessary purchase. It is not worth the trouble to use most of the time. I could have lived simpler, but everybody else has a fancy vacuum, and they told me on the television that it was the way to go, and so I vacuum.

You don't need a boat; you just want to go fishing. You don't need a house; you just need a safe place to sleep, eat, and relax. You don't need a stove, a microwave, a double oven, a toaster, a waffle iron, a grill, a hot plate, a crock-pot, an electric skillet, and a turkey fryer; you just want a good hot meal. You don't need 2 cars, an SUV, a road bike, a street bike, roller blades, skateboards, and an off road motorcycle; you just need to get over *there* once in a while. You don't need to save millions of dollars for retirement, if you are not going to do anything of value with your life in your 20's and 30's and 40's. I mean what's the point? If you didn't do much while you were young, do you really think you are going to care how much money you have in the bank when you are old and can barely walk? The list goes go on and on and on.

Cultivate *material aversion*. Can you see how much more powerful you are *when you can live happily without* the 900 square foot addition to your house and without the $20,000 kitchen remodel job, and without the second car?

The modern day word describing the problem is "affluenza". It comes from combining the two words *affluence* and *influenza*. Affluenza is a painful, contagious, socially transmitted condition of overload, debt, anxiety, and waste resulting from the dogged pursuit of more. It creates a bloated, sluggish and unfulfilled feeling that results from efforts to keep up with others. It causes an epidemic of stress, overwork, waste and indebtedness done in the name of the *pursuit of the American Dream*. On a global scale it is an unsustainable addiction to economic growth.

Flee affluenza, thereby freeing yourself. Do this before it's too late. The pursuit of endless increases in material wealth leads to feelings of worthlessness and dissatisfaction rather than a *better life*. These symptoms appear like those of a physical disease. Many of those who become wealthy find the economic success leaves them unfulfilled and hungrier than ever for even more wealth. They are unable to get pleasure from the things they buy. Then the study of how to get even more stuff begins to dominate their time and thoughts. Their personal relationships decline. They are no longer happy nor can they remember what it feels like to be happy. The condition is considered particularly acute amongst those with inherited wealth, who are often said to experience guilt, lack of purpose and dissolute behavior, as well as an obsession with holding on to the wealth.

When you free your time and location by Vanaboding you will automatically have at least five times more money. WHY? Because you reduce your overhead to almost nothing. Compare paying $3,200 a month in living expenses holed up in the big city, working 50 hours a week after commuting 10 hours a week to spending $600 a month Vanaboding and having almost EVERY SECOND TO YOUR SELF! Being able to exercise your free will is what separates those that have been traditionally identified as being rich from those that truly ARE rich. If you don't own your time you don't own anything, I don't care how much money you have in the bank. If you use your money to buy more things, instead of buying your life back, you are committing an unforgivable crime against yourself. "Spending the best part of your life earning money in order to enjoy a questionable time later during the least valuable part of it (if you even make it to retirement) is stupid", paraphrased from the master Thoreau in his seminal work *Walden*.

Many ask "what will I have to give up if I Vanabode?" My answer, "You will give up nothing of importance. You will gain everything. You will do more; with less stress and money than you ever dreamed". More importantly, I ask you, "What will you sacrifice if you continue on the path you are on right now? What are you giving up to live the life you are currently living?"

Ask yourself, "what would I be doing right now, and tomorrow, and next week *if I could?*" The answer will most likely *not* be piddling around your house with all the junk you have bought. So start by selling what you don't need. This means you will probably sell almost everything you own. What it boils down to is determining exactly what you really need and then finding the simplest, fastest, easiest, and cheapest solution to getting there. I have done this for you.

Simply acquire everything described in the **Inventory** chapter and put it to use as described throughout this book to travel in perpetuity. Do not add anything major to the list. Do not purchase any additional complicated devices. Do not deviate from the list unless you have a real reason, or specific need that I have not addressed. The acquisition and implementation of these tools and strategies will provide you with a simple, unencumbered life while traveling comfortably in an uncrowded vehicle. You will enjoy all the *Essentials of a Great Life:* excellent food, great sleep, good personal hygiene, healthy sex, and protection from the elements. For more on *simplification* see the **Budget** and the **Fun** chapters.

The Van

To Vanabode is to live and travel easier, safer, longer and cheaper than any other method. The single greatest piece of equipment needed for this lifestyle is your vehicle. It will be your transportation and your place of rest. I have tried traveling and living in nearly everything else. Concerning the few methods I have not *personally* tried; I consulted with those who have, to find out their shortcomings. I have done extensive research to discover the pitfalls of them all: including houseboats, tractor trailers, yachts, underground houses, bus conversions like the movie stars use, fifth wheel trailers, school buses, motor homes, backpack supported tent camping, hostels, hotels, car camping, resorts, and old unfaithful: the mortgage supported single family home, condo, or town home.

No other method of travel living compares to Vanaboding. If Vanaboding is not cheaper than some other method then it ends up being more fun. If it is not more comfortable then it ends up being easier. If it is not easier then it turns out to be more sustainable, meaning you can do it longer.

The choice of this exact van over every other vehicle choice is deceptively simple but supremely important. Vanaboding on a super low budget and having a lot of fun doing it usually requires that you use the correct kind of van outfitted for mobility, sleeping and safety, and that you follow my advice for living strategies.

I recommend a van exactly like the one seen in this picture. Rent it, buy it, trade your car for it, or borrow one for as long as you need to. You can still use many of the travel techniques outlined in this book even if you choose to car camp, choose to travel in a motorhome, or choose some other inferior mode of transportation. However, you will not have the same level of success you could have had, if you simply followed my recommendations on this particular point.

Notice the van is plain white, non-attention grabbing, with no external indications that someone is using it for housing or camping. There are no roof racks, stove or hot water heater vents, bicycle racks, or RV style windows. My Vanabode does not have a raised roof. It is the standard wheelbase not the extended super long wheelbase type. It looks like hundreds of thousands of other work vans used all over the country because that's what it is.

We have windows only in the back doors but they do not open; this gives us extra privacy, security, and most importantly, less attention. It looks like a work van, not a camping van. This one deceptively simple choice will buy you a ton of privacy and hassle free nights. You will be able to sleep for free in places you never dreamed possible.

Notice we chose a sliding side door rather than the hinged swing out kind. This is good for getting in and out with large objects like our bed mattress and cooler, and makes it easier to open in close quarters. This makes it easier to leave open for beautiful unobstructed views of the ocean or mountains without concern that the wind will blow it shut.

The bed is a super high quality pillow top mattress purchased from a normal retail store and then mounted on two sheets of 3/4" plywood supported by 2" x 4" studs sitting atop 2 commercial gray storage cabinets. Notice the clear plastic storage containers under the bed, which pull out easily. They contain clothes, tools, dry foods, toiletries, etc. The toilet is seen in this photo as well stored for easy access under the bed. Pictures are included here in the book. On the website there are more details, questions and answers from customers, and discussions about construction. People needlessly obsess over the exact layout. Most of the additional dialogue is over issues people would not have if they simply followed my advice.

The van is 6 feet wide on the inside as long as you do not install interior sidewalls. The pegboard shown on the sidewall in one picture here did not work well. It took up space and provided little in return. I removed it. The bare metal sidewalls are roomier, easier to attach bungee cords to for securing various things, and easier to keep clean. I recommend you get the standard van with the simple rubber floor because carpet and other fancier flooring gets dirty too easily and becomes an allergen. Rubber floors make dry or wet clean up easy.

This van has a short wheelbase. Long wheel base extended version vans give you more room inside, but they are harder to park in the big city parking garages in places like New York City, Chicago, San Francisco and Las Vegas. If you are *only* visiting the outback or off road locations and do not intend to spend time in museums, big cities, art galleries, etc. then the longer van is okay. However when visiting any kind of city, especially those in California and those on the East Coast, longer vans prevent you from doing many activities due to expensive ticket enforced parking restrictions. They can also be unsafe at highway speeds and burn more fuel.

ALL other vehicles are inferior to this set up. High top vehicles prevent you from parking in big city parking garages or passing through a simple drive through. Cars and minivans are too small. RV's and motor homes tell the world that you are camping and therefore cannot be traveled in long term for less than $50 a day unless you stay off grid, in the wild open bush, and out of the paid campgrounds at least 90% of the time. Big RV's burn too much gas. They make it difficult to sleep anywhere without paying to be in a campground. They limit your exploring to those established official campgrounds and the *time it takes to get to them.*

We once lived and traveled out of a gorgeous 34 foot diesel Class A motorhome. We were always running into serious limitations on where we could go, what we could do, and how long we could stay there. Sure they are comfortable once you settle in and get them set up. But that is part of the point. We don't want to settle in to one boring place with a hundred other camp fire burning, kid smacking, dog barking, noisy, weekend warrior, motorhome owners bickering over who has the best awning or the drunkest husband.

We were in southern California once for a 40 day exploration before heading north and we had to stay a 70 minute drive from the beaches that we wanted to see. Why? Because our motorhome was too big to park securely anywhere near the ocean. So every day we climbed out of our motorhome, got in the car we pulled behind us and drove in heavy traffic to get beachside. We did this for 20 days. Then we did the same thing all over the city, visiting botanical gardens, wine tasting shops, art galleries, zoos and parks.

Why was that so bad? We gave up all the conveniences of the motorhome because we no longer had it with us throughout the day. It was just sitting there 70 miles away costing us $46 a day in campground fees. We could not use the bathroom in it, take a shower, rest for an hour, make lunch, or anything else. Our overall budget ended up being nearly $97 a day because of all the extra running around, distance from our food, and camping costs. It forced us to spend a minimum of 3 hours a day in traffic in a small cramped car. We had to load and unload everything we thought we might need for the day and of course we always forgot something.

I knew there was a better way. Vanabode was born. Since then we have taken countless runs through those same areas using our properly outfitted van with zero hassle, on less than $20 a day, with no extra driving, no camping fees, safely and securely. We see nearly twice what we used to see in half the time opening up other exploratory options.

Make sure you have a matching full size spare tire. The smaller "donut" tires will not work for you in an off road situation where you need to quickly get back on the road after a flat tire. For example, we were off-roading on a dirt rock strewn road through Death Valley. We hit a rock just the wrong way and it ripped through one of our tires. I simply changed the tire and we continued our trip uninterrupted. We lost 2 hours.

When we got back to Las Vegas *4 days later* I bought a suitable replacement cheaply from Wal-Mart. If we only had the miniature spare tire it would have been very different. It would have ruined our trip. Why? Cell phones were not working to call for help because we were in the middle of nowhere. The donut tires are too small to drive off road with so we would have had to end our trip right there. A tow vehicle would have been over $400 due to the remote location *even if we could have reached someone*. We had none of these troubles because our van was properly outfitted with the full size properly inflated spare tire.

If you cannot acquire a van like the one I recommend, you can still use this guide to help save money and provide valuable insights into where to go in your car or motorhome: just don't expect to do it as effortlessly or as cheaply. You certainly cannot go everywhere we have gone if you choose a *larger* vehicle. For instance, they don't care if you're sleeping in your car or a 45 foot bus in Laughlin, Nevada (a place I highly recommend for a month or two by the way). However if you take that big camper or bus sized RV to San Francisco or most anywhere in California you better have the money to play the campground game at $50-$140 a night.

You could complete about 75% of our travels using a specialty vehicle like a class B camping van. The problem is it will cost you a whole lot more unless you do *not* visit the big cities. These smaller class b camper vans are just like the big RV's when it comes to city environments. You will not be able to stay anywhere you want because the local authorities know you are camping. They will usually harass you or ticket you until you leave, and then you will have to find and pay for a campground somewhere.

If you plan on spending nearly all of your time legally camping on the BLM wilderness type lands then you do not need to use a van just like mine. You can skip the stealth strategies outlined in this book when camping in order to save money. You can allow for the big motorhome or class B camper van. This gives you more room and comfort but obviously costs more money. The moment you choose a vehicle other than a true Vanabode you will give up many *other* things, some you won't even realize until later.

If you are not convinced consult the **Vanabode Versus Other Living Strategies** chapter. It contains comparisons of Vanaboding to all other methods of travel and living including the good and bad involved in backpacking, air travel with hotel rooms, car travel, large motor homes, RV's or travel trailers, living in a house, living on a boat, being homeless, and more.

Image shows the easy access via the double-hinged 50/50 back doors. Curtains cover the windows when not driving, and items stored under the bed are easy to reach from outside.

I do not waste time, money or interior room on insulation. You don't really insulate a vehicle against the outside temperatures like you do a house anyway. You instead end up trapping the very temperature you don't want inside. The actual insulation in a heavily insulated van gets hot while you are off somewhere and will take more hours to cool down when you return. The actual insulation also freezes in the cold and takes longer to warm up when the sun comes out. Most insulation is toxic especially when heated and cooled every single day for the life of the vehicle. I also like to hear what is going on outside my Vanabode while sleeping. I love the sounds of wildlife at night. I also want to hear anyone approaching my van when I am sleeping. Heavy insulation makes that more difficult. So avoid it.

Great views out the back doors from the bed help make camping like this a dream. We often easily see wildlife with the double back doors open when we just lie real still even though it feels like we are in plain view. The interior of the van is so dark they don't seem to get spooked. You can also take great pictures from this vantage point.

We chose the Chevy Express 2500 van with the large V8 engine. You can save about $2,000 by purchasing the same size van with the V6 engine and it gets about 1 mile per gallon better fuel mileage. However, the V6 is harder to sell when you are done with it because nearly all service and construction companies prefer the bigger engine for longevity and towing power. When we trade for a newer van someday we will more seriously consider the V6 version with its better fuel mileage. At our age it may be the last one we ever have to purchase meaning resale value is meaningless.

I bought mine through the fleet manager at a Chevy dealership. He accepted my Consumer Reports print out of the acceptable price to pay. He did not haggle me or turn a nagging salesman loose on me intent on an upsell. If you need to save money always buy used, preferably a certified preowned vehicle with less than 40% of its expected life gone. I could sell my van tomorrow to any number of millions of tradesmen that work from vehicles like it. By contrast it can take a year or more to sell a motor home or specialized RV because the market is so much smaller for such vehicles. This is another reason to Vanabode rather than RV. It enables you to get in and out of the market if you need to, quickly and easily, while experiencing the least risk and depreciation.

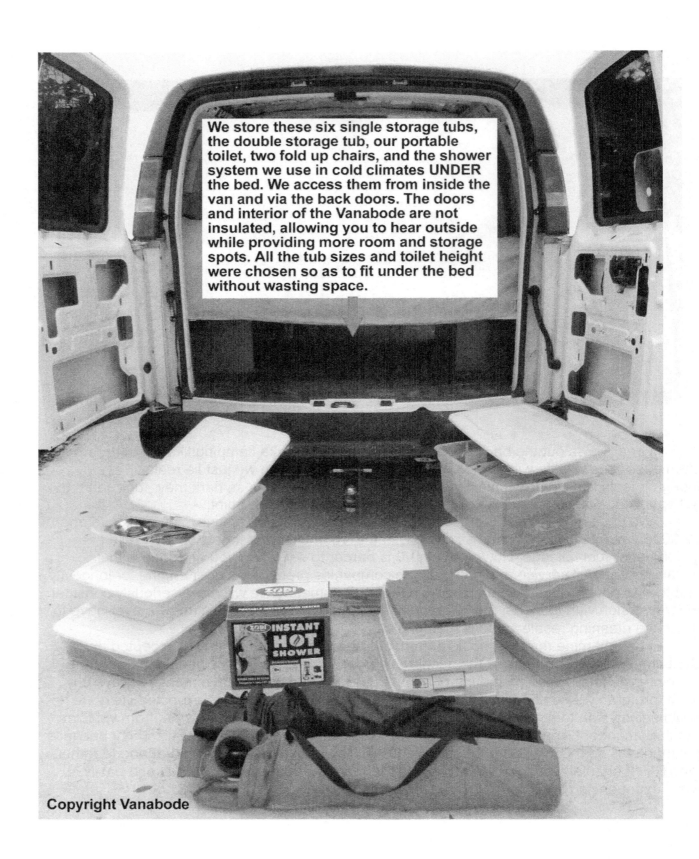

We store these six single storage tubs, the double storage tub, our portable toilet, two fold up chairs, and the shower system we use in cold climates UNDER the bed. We access them from inside the van and via the back doors. The doors and interior of the Vanabode are not insulated, allowing you to hear outside while providing more room and storage spots. All the tub sizes and toilet height were chosen so as to fit under the bed without wasting space.

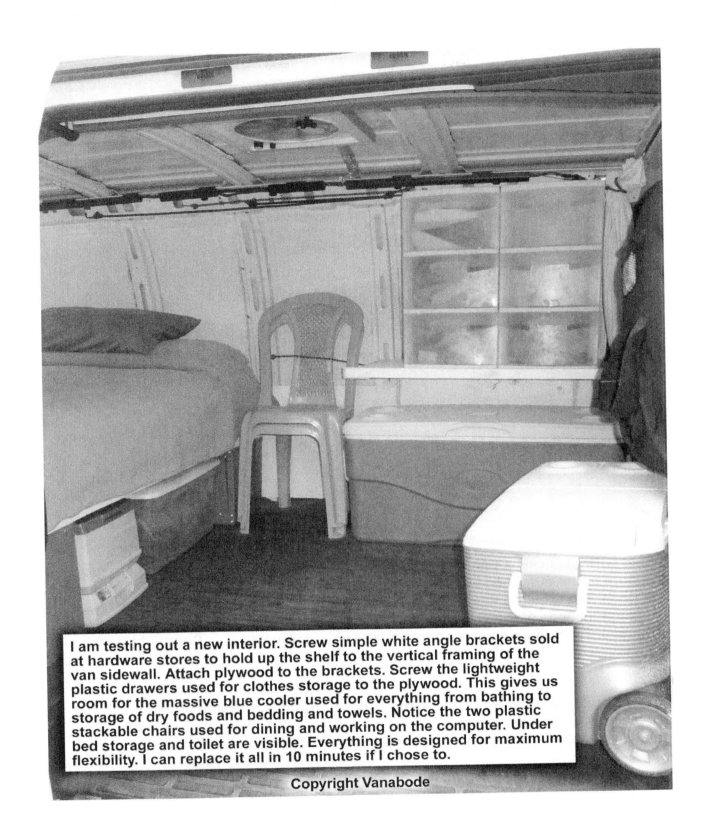

I am testing out a new interior. Screw simple white angle brackets sold at hardware stores to hold up the shelf to the vertical framing of the van sidewall. Attach plywood to the brackets. Screw the lightweight plastic drawers used for clothes storage to the plywood. This gives us room for the massive blue cooler used for everything from bathing to storage of dry foods and bedding and towels. Notice the two plastic stackable chairs used for dining and working on the computer. Under bed storage and toilet are visible. Everything is designed for maximum flexibility. I can replace it all in 10 minutes if I chose to.

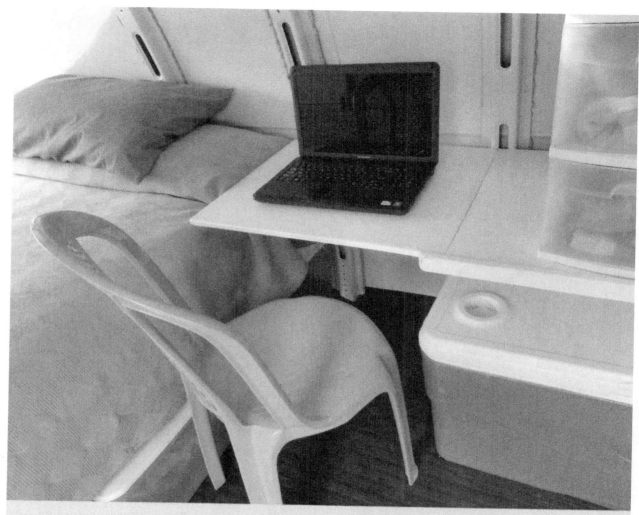

This portable desk is part of the new interior design we are using. Compare this picture to the other one with the chairs strapped to the wall to get an idea of how it is done. The tabletop is a single piece of plywood that is stored behind the chairs against the side of the van, then set on top of the shelf and rested on the pillow on the bed. You can eat there or interact with your computer.   Copyright Vanabode

For more pictures and details on the interior layout and construction visit Vanabode construction details on the Internet.
(http://www.vanabode.com/camp/construction-details.htm).

Essentials of a Great Life

This chapter is an overview of one of the most important elements in this book. If you skip over any part of this you will probably fail. If you discount any one of the essential ingredients to traveling successfully listed below, you will never achieve long-term satisfaction and the complete feeling of romantic travel. I cannot stress this enough. Those that skip any one of these will suffer and blame their travel mates, or their budget, or their health or something other than what it really is: the failure to understand the importance of these fine points of living on the road.

Many people "go camping" when they are young. The people that try to *camp* rarely understand any of the principles I outline in this book. I hear them all the time "I don't like camping. My idea of camping is a hotel room with a TV and a hair dryer". When I ask them why they don't like camping they can't even answer me. Why? Because they don't even know. They usually defensively state, "I don't know, I just don't like it". Sometimes they realize exactly why they had a bad experience. "I hate being dirty all the time", or "the food sucked", or "it was too hot, too rainy, too tiring", or "so many bugs got into the tent".

So, why did a potentially great and wonderful experience turn out poorly? The answer is simple. They did not adequately address the *Essentials of a Great Life*. Of course they did not enjoy being dirty, or hungry, or tired, or wet or cold. Who does? Vanabode provides the proper action plan to simply, easily and cheaply deal with all the issues pertaining to extended travel. I will even show you how to happily live without a house altogether, forever, if you like. Thoroughly implement this book and you will have the most incredible, exciting, romantic experiences of your life. We have, and still are, after 20+ years of marriage.

The Essentials of a Great Life are: *excellent food, great sleep, good personal hygiene, healthy sex,* and *protection from the elements.* Your goal is to find your personal synergy in these elements that leads you to complete harmony. Each elements success depends on the others. For example, you won't have *fun* if you don't get enough *sleep*. You won't get good *sleep* if you aren't *clean*. You won't have great *sex* if you are dehydrated out in the icy cold pouring rain not *protected from the elements*. And you won't care about any of it if you are *hungry*. Get them all in place while traveling and you will experience life as you have never lived it. Romantic. Extreme. Unforgettable.

Some describe this blissful harmony as nirvana, heaven, being whole, being at peace, being satisfied, being happy, or being complete. It is the smooth quiet comfortable feeling of having attained something pure. You will not want to be anywhere else. Once you get set up correctly it will be nearly effortless. You will not be dreaming and wishing and hoping things will get better because they already are better. You will feel like you have arrived, because you have. You will be happy. Most people have never experienced this level of fulfillment for longer than a couple of days. While Vanaboding and living anywhere you choose; you can attain this permanently. Then, life's long-term prospects get very exciting indeed.

The Vanabode lifestyle is very conducive to developing a satisfying life, whether you do it in short bursts like a week every 3 months or so, or better yet, for 90 days or longer at a time. My wife and I have lived from an RV or van for many years without a house. We are currently in our late 40's and are finally up for a new kind of challenge. We are planning a 50 mile a day Vanabode run up the East Coast from Florida to the Canadian border with months spent in Washington DC, Chicago, and the other surrounding super expensive cities seeing the hundreds of galleries, museums, and government buildings. We want to make sure it can be done on $20 a day. Realize you can't even park in some of these places for less than $25 a day. So, it will be quite a challenge. Make sure you are on the mailing list so we can keep you updated on the day to day details. We will be creating a separate Destination Guide (http://www.vanabode.com/travel/destinations.htm) on the website for each day of the trip so you can see how to do it, where we suggest going and what we suggest avoiding.

We have such comfortable nearly effortless travel time, and like it so much long term, because we implement the following *Essentials of a Great Life* (compare my list against Maslow's hierarchy of needs). I have listed each one below with a short explanation. Chapters covering each element in detail follow.

Great Food is one of the single most important issues to a fun vacation style life. Enjoy a wide variety of food affordably by choosing fresh, healthy, flavorful, organically grown foods from farmers markets and fine restaurants all over the United States. The **Food** chapter covers food storage, purchase strategies, choices, budget, kitchenware, inventory, how to determine whether a restaurant is a good risk or not, and more.

Great Sleep cannot be emphasized enough. The **Sleep** chapter covers what it takes to rest good in your own clean bed every night, quietly and safely. I will show you why this is very important to successful traveling.

Good Personal Hygiene must be maintained or you will feel like you are on a temporary camping trip rather than living a complete healthy life. Do not skimp here. You don't have to. I will show you how to do it all including bathing, showering, shaving, using the bathroom, clean ups, and more while seeing the country via road trip.

Healthy Sex depends on your relationship with your travel mate, eating and sleeping well, being clean, and having fun. Some short-term travelers put their sex life on hold *until they get back home.* This is a mistake. When you are traveling you *are* home. You live *in* your body remember? I include some sex tips while Vanaboding and why you should plan for enjoying yourself anywhere you choose.

Protection from the Elements is fairly self-explanatory. When it is raining, snowing, storming, too hot, too cold, too sunny, too scary, too noisy, or too windy, you just want to get out of it all. You need a safe, clean, quiet neutral place to *be.* Your Vanabode provides this with the least amount of commitment and cost.

Food

    Eating well is one of the top *Essentials of a Great Life.* If you skimp here nobody in your group will be happy, your journey will be a disappointment, and it will probably end early with complaints like, "I think I'll just stay home next time". In America we neglect the fine art of eating and dining. Our families are distant because we don't take the time to do it right. America is fat and unhealthy as well because we don't *enjoy eating* like we should. It has been proven in various studies that mealtimes with friends and family are very important to a person's overall happiness. Plan for and enjoy at *least* one long 2-3 hour meal weekly with people you like.

    Picture shows a sample Vanabode lunch including fresh grapefruit, sesame crackers, dates, and cheese soaked in olive oil over snow peas, avocado, and heirloom tomatoes.

Even though we cook a lot of meals for ourselves, eating healthy raw foods like this straight from the farmers markets and stored in our cooler is hard to beat.

Eating more raw foods will make you healthier; sometimes almost instantly. Raw foods are easy to digest, don't require cooking or cleanup, and often don't require refrigeration or complicated storage solutions. Raw foods can be cheaper, and if you factor in the health benefits they are absolutely the best thing you can do to eliminate disease and increase your lifespan. This has been proven over and over with hundreds of clinical trials by the scientific and medical professions. See Joel Fuhrman's extraordinary works *Eat to Live* and also *Super Immunity* found in the BOOK portion of the Vanabode Travel Store (http://www.vanabode.com/camp/amazon-travel-store.htm). Essentially your diet should mostly consist of fresh fruits and vegetables with beans, seeds and nuts for healthy proteins.

Today everyone eats nearly anemic foods. People eat 2 to 3 times *more* food today than they did 100 years ago because the food is almost devoid of real nutrition. We eat a greater quantity of calories, but are actually starving for nutrition, thus the obesity, cancer, and diabetes plagues. Today's foods have been sprayed and sometimes drenched in pesticides. It has been morphed and changed via monoculturistic breeding born out of the genetically modified organism movement. The GMO system focuses on giving farmers products they can easily grow, ship and store without regard to real nutritional content. So, most Americans end up eating cardboard calories, useless filler with calories sprayed on at the last minute as it goes out the door.

Obesity, diabetes, cancers and other diseases are a huge problem because our bodies are screaming *for nutrition, not calories,* but we don't know the difference. Big commercial food companies grow oversized, attractive, consistently sized food items from bad soil so they can make money. They have no incentive to produce anything that has a higher percentage of real nutritional value, because our society does not know how to buy food based on nutritional content.

My Vanabode lifestyle encourages the opposite. Buy and eat raw local organic foods from farmers markets in the area you are traveling through. Eliminate garbage food from your life. Remove the middleman. Avoid packaged food *products.*

Also, we have allowed technology to hinder us rather than make us better people. For instance, when the microwave was first being sold it was marketed as a huge help for the time strapped housewife or household cook. It was supposed to make it easier to make meals, and therefore give our families more time together.

It did not. Our busy society simply used it to *speed up cooking.* We missed the point. We did not successfully improve our lives. Now our families don't even eat together. Each party just heats up some convoluted blob of manufactured food byproducts or a frozen dinner and eats alone. Each person does this whenever they feel like it, because there is no need for a designated mealtime. We eat without a word to the others in our house like a rat eating a piece of garbage. Then we each going our own way not connecting at all.

We have neglected the really important issues of food consumption. Eating is not about wolfing down some mediocre bunch of empty calories in front of the television. Meals should be romantic. Instead we eat whatever is in the fridge and whatever can be heated up *quickly.* Why? Because we are too tired from work to do or care otherwise.

When you eat you should taste the food and relish the intricate flavors. Smell the food. Take in each ingredients special aroma. Experience the texture of each individual item. The French typically take over 90 minutes to enjoy a well-paced dinner and nice conversation whereas most Americans get by on less than 15 minutes.

Sometimes we literally stuff our face while steering our car through traffic, noise and pollution. Eating should be fun, not a chore. It should offer time for everyone to sit face to face and discuss important and interesting things: to find out what is going on in our family. Instead each person just chokes down the ingredients and runs back to the computer or television or other mindless empty distraction. It is a shame that our garbage disposals eat better than most of the world's children, and yet still we don't truly enjoy our meals that often.

You should be able to *look forward to eating* because you *know* it is going to be one of the nicest experiences of the day. Done correctly, eating on the road can be fantastic fun. It will enhance and improve your life, health and attitude towards others. You can eat better, more often, cheaper, and healthier while Vanaboding than via any other lifestyle. You will be able to afford first class food. You will have the time to find and prepare it. You will have the time to enjoy it.

The **Inventory** chapter contains a complete list of food related items to bring when Vanaboding including coolers, stoves, utensils, and tools. Here I will cover various strategies for eating healthy and fun, cleaning up, food storage, cooking, locating and purchasing good food, farmers markets, choosing good restaurants, and free products. Some of my advice involves keeping it cheap while other advice is about saving time or getting higher quality. Decide what is most important to you and disregard the rest.

Food storage is one of the most important areas to address. You can wear the same clothes week after week but you can't eat the same food over and over. Once it's gone it's gone. Our basic strategy is to store about a weeks' worth of nonperishable food in one of the plastic storage tubs, and store about a weeks' worth of perishable food in our cooler. Then we eat nearly everything else fresh as soon as we buy it from farmers markets and roadside vendors. Once you get out and about and off the interstates you will find lots of people selling what they grow. Fresh fruit, vegetables, and items like dried meats and cheeses keep quite well in the cooler in the van. If you go off grid for 3-4 weeks at a time simply bring more canned or dry stored foods to suit your needs.

Ice lasts longer in a full cooler. On longer trips where it gets very hot during the day the cost of ice can get prohibitive. Who wants to stop what they are doing, spend an hour and $8 in gas driving 30 miles to a store to buy $5 worth of ice to keep $4 worth of food cold? This is not a good use of time or money. People ate and flourished for thousands of years without refrigeration. So can you if need be.

Purchase a cooler that has a luggage style handle and wheels for rolling around, a drain in the bottom, and a split lid so you don't have to open the entire thing when reaching in to just grab an apple off the top. The one we have has cup holders built into the top so when we sit in the van and eat it holds our drinks too. It is also sturdy enough to sit on when the occasion presents itself.

You can place your cooler on top of a thick piece of foam insulation like the kind used in furniture. You can purchase scrap pieces from upholstery shops or use a pillow or heavy blankets underneath. This further insulates the cooler and food from the outside hot air under the van and also from the engine, transmission and exhaust heat when driving. You can also use another piece of insulation, foam, pillow, or bedding for the top. We don't do this because it gets in our way when accessing the cooler or sitting on top of it.

Purchase high quality sealable plastic or glass storage containers that fit tight in your cooler and have super tight sealing lids. Pack each one full and close the lid tightly keeping items that need to be coldest at the bottom. You do not want any water touching your food. This is especially true for fruits and vegetables. Water contact will make them smell strange and rot them faster. We leave the ice-cold water from the melted ice in the cooler until the ice is completely melted. We then drain it into a jug for bathing our feet or rinsing dishes.

Dry foods like crackers, nuts, seeds, meat jerkies, breads, and even some cheeses do just fine in a zip lock in a cool shaded part of the van. We use some canned goods as a backup food source and we store them in the plastic storage containers under the bed. Honestly though, we hardly ever eat out of a can because, even though it is easy, it is not as nutritious or fun as eating fresh foods.

Locating and purchasing groceries has never been difficult while Vanaboding. You can buy locally grown foods from vendors and farmers markets all over the country. It is cheaper, healthier, more fun and easier to do than scheduling a big restaurant sitting. These small places usually offer cheap nutritious food. When you first come into a town or area stop and ask if there are any farmers markets, local farm outlets, or places that sell fresh locally grown foods. Then plan to visit if it fits your schedule. Usually they are open on Friday, Saturday and Sunday but some stay open all week for short hours each day.

My wife likes this so much we often plan visiting a specialty market as the central activity for the day, followed by lunch at a local park and a fresh dinner supplemented with an interesting bottle of locally made wine or cider. See the "farmer's market finder" on the important external websites page of the website. (http://www.vanabode.com/camp/links.htm). This site will allow you to search and locate thousands of local markets in every state.

Having *time* to shop may be hard to get used to at first. Most people in their normal lives have almost no time for grocery shopping. They don't consider it a pleasure, but rather a chore. They rush through traffic, fight the crowds at the large bulk discount store and buy huge quantities of whatever will keep for long periods of time and hope they don't have to come back to the crowded stores again for a week or two.

While Vanaboding though, you will have a great time shopping because you have the time and money to buy the best. You can hand check each piece of fruit, buy only in season for the tastiest examples, and take your time wandering around the various stores and local markets all over the country. It can be a lot of fun even for a guy. Why? Because you have the *time* to do it. You are not rushed to get done so you can get to work or any number of other distracting boring tiring duties. You can enjoy the time while choosing each item you will nourish your body with. You can be present, right there in that moment.

Stop and talk to those working in the shop. Taste the free samples. Investigate the subtle nuances of the local fare. Don't be in a hurry. Relax and get the best for your money. Most times we only buy enough for two to three days. Then we get to fun shop again, somewhere different. When traveling heavily populated areas like California or Florida, sometimes my wife and I will only buy enough for two days. We have fun shopping three or four days a week for the best selection, variety and price.

Choosing good restaurants can be fun too. My wife and I tend to splurge here. We spend too much money eating great prepared meals everywhere we go. But if you are on a stricter budget you don't have to. Nearly every city, regardless of how small, has some kind of lunch buffet usually priced at $5 to $8 each. I know some people who only eat one meal a day and they seem quite satisfied. Many people make the mistake of thinking they need a lot of food, so many calories, when in reality they just need a small, low calorie portion of highly nutritious food.

Experiencing each communities unique and interesting cuisine is a huge part of fun travel. We take the time to do this everywhere we go unless we are on particularly tight budget. Have you ever had the famous deep-fried Twinkie in downtown Vegas? When was the last time you savored a rich, lean buffalo burger smothered in a smoldering musky deep brown mushroom sauce at a Wyoming ranch? Have you tasted Baltimore's most incredibly succulent made fresh daily crab cakes? What about the pungent earthy sourdough baked fresh each morning in San Francisco? I have tasted these and each new discovery was a wonderful experience. Savor these moments. Enjoy the establishment's ambience and your travel mates company.

When picking one place over ten others, work down a list of priorities. First the two of you should discuss what kind of food you think you want. Will it be Japanese sushi, urban grub, authentic Mexican or succulent seafood tonight? Then pick a budget. Then discuss how far you are willing to drive to get it. Then consult local authorities like welcome centers or travel shops. You can ask anyone for an opinion on where to eat, from the guy returning the shopping carts at the grocery store to the President of the United States.

Ask *specific* questions to get information you can really use. For example, if you have decided on Mexican and a $20 budget for two, ask "where can I get a delicious Mexican meal for about $10 a plate within ten miles of here?" instead of "are there any restaurants around here?" Don't get discouraged if you don't get the information you need on the first try. People are so far removed from where they "live" that they often have no idea how to answer. They say they "live" there but really do nothing more than work, sleep and watch television. Many don't have the time or money to go out. Ask ten people, if that is what it takes, to get the best restaurant lined up for your exciting dinner out.

Cooking can be done using a variety of tools including my personal favorite; the solar oven. You can also use a 12-volt oven, campfire, mini wood fired stove, propane or liquid gas camping stove, or even a blowtorch. See the EQUIPMENT category of the Vanabode Travel Store (http://www.vanabode.com/camp/amazon-travel-store.htm). Each method has distinct advantages and disadvantages in terms of cost, safety and ease of use. On a 7 day trip through various cities we typically end up eating about 5 hot meals in restaurants, 4 hot self-cooked meals using either the solar oven, 12 volt oven or propane camping stove, and the rest of the meals consist of fresh, raw fruits and vegetables and cold foods like breakfast cereals. Let me be clear here. We never, ever, travel without eating well. Eating great meals is one of the most important elements in the *Essentials of a Great Life.*

Solar Oven - you can use a solar oven to cook anywhere for free without electricity, smoke, wood, fire or fuel. The solar oven works best in sunnier areas. Most anything can be easily cooked in 3 hours. Some items in full sun are done in 30 minutes. Most people using the solar oven, load it with food, angle it so it will be in the most sun when they *return* from hiking or work, then go for a 3 hour walk in the woods. When they get back the roast, baked potatoes and bread are hot and ready to eat. If you have never laid back in your lawn chair with song birds carrying on all around you, the smell of a nice little 6 ounce rib eye sizzling in the oven at your feet, and sipped a glass of cool wine after a long hike through the gorgeous wild countryside, then I'd say you are missing out.

I have written 3 full web pages on his fantastic free way to cook using a solar oven. (http://www.vanabode.com/camp/solar-oven-cooking.htm) The only disadvantages to this high quality oven are: 1) even though it is light and easy to carry it is bigger than a camp stove, 2) it cannot be used in the dark, 3) it cannot be set up in high winds. It fits easily in the van as it should, but if you don't plan on doing your own cooking you may opt to use it only at your residence. Picture shows a delicious meal of scalloped potatoes broiling in our sun oven.

Camp Fire - some people just cannot have fun unless they can cook and play with an open fire. Many of the best places we have been still allow campfires but it varies from place to place and often changes depending on the weather and time of year. You can never totally depend on being able to have an open fire for cooking. Sometimes it rains. Sometimes it is too windy. Sometimes it is illegal due to wild fire restrictions that change from one day to the next. Sometimes you can't find firewood. If you want to cook over a fire be careful, burn pain lasts a long time, and don't burn down a national forest. Penalties are severe.

Propane Gas Stove - when my wife is not using the solar oven she prefers the simple little one burner camping stove for one pot meals. The one shown in the picture incorporates pot sizes that nest inside each other. It is simple to set up and lights and burns easily. It is cheap to operate and inexpensive to purchase. It takes up little room in the van. The one we have has never failed to light. However it can be difficult to get enough heat from the open flame to quickly cook anything when it is windy.

If both people in the party cook each can have their own stove and cook their meal just the way they like it. Do not set it up this kind of stove anywhere near the vehicle where it

could cause an explosion. Never pull over and jump out of the van only to find it windy and then snuggle your open fire stove right up to the exhaust pipe of the van. Do not store the propane fuel canister anywhere it gets hot. It is an explosive fuel. If it were to explode it could kill anyone in the van or nearby. We keep the fuel under the bed, each canister wrapped separately in a small towel to prevent motion abrasion that could damage the propane cylinder wall.

Sometimes we go on long city-based trips where we do not cook at all. We eat cold cereal or fruit for breakfast or just drink a cup of coffee and have a donut. Then for lunch we eat fresh bread dipped in an olive oil, salt and spice mix. We have specialty goat cheese or sheep cheese, crackers, olives, raw vegetables like carrots, onions, tomatoes, broccoli, and salad greens with balsamic vinegar for dressing. Then we finish it off with a locally purchased sweet roll or cookie for dessert. We end the day at a restaurant with an early dinner if we want early bird prices. Sometimes we eat a very late dinner if it is hot out and we don't want to be in the van as soon as it gets dark.

Stainless Steel Mini Stove - you can use simple twigs and scrap wood to power this incredible tiny portable stainless steel mini stove. It folds and stores flat. It boils water in minutes using almost no wood due to the super simple easy to feed design. This stove will last forever. It is so small and light it can easily be carried in a large pocket or backpack for cooking while out away from the van hiking. Find it in the EQUIPMENT part of the Vanabode Travel Store (http://www.vanabode.com/camp/amazon-travel-store.htm)

Torch - you can actually brown up a hotdog in one minute using a simple propane powered blow torch you see used on the cooking shows. I personally don't do this much as we tend to eat together and the oven and stove seems to do a better more well-rounded job of cooking larger more complicated dishes. Also, even though they are supposed to be safe, standing there holding this can of explosive gas with fire shooting out the end has never made me very comfortable. If you are eating alone though you can heat up a can of beans in 5 minutes using the torch and eat right out of the can. This is one of the easiest and fastest, methods to cook a one dish meal and eliminate dishes altogether.

12 volt ovens are one of the absolute best, cheapest, and easiest methods of cooking. Over the road truckers use them daily to cook hot meals while they are driving down the road. You can use the oven even when the van is not running though. The one I show in the EQUIPMENT part of the Vanabode Travel Store (http://www.vanabode.com/camp/amazon-travel-store.htm) is the best one for longevity, ease of use, and cooking power.

12-volt microwaves are used by some people. Some claim you can use one of these while van traveling and eliminate the need for any other kind of cooking device or system. I see them for sale on the Internet for $250 and up. I have read reviews about them taking 5-7 minutes to pop a bag of popcorn. I see that big name brand companies typically do not sell them. These issues concern me. Since we have been happy with the other cooking methods outlined previously, we have not had the need to try one.

After discovering Fuhrman's extraordinary work on eating to transform your health without medicine, we have moved to eating more raw foods. This philosophy is perfect for Vanaboding. We eat healthier, cheaper, with reduced preparation time, without cooking or needing a power source, and eliminate most dish washing chores. His strategies also empower greater independence. Now we are satisfied without restaurant meals for much longer periods of time. Find Fuhrman's work in the BOOK portion of the Vanabode Travel Store (http://www.vanabode.com/camp/amazon-travel-store.htm)

These foods are exceptionally good while traveling because they are tasty, nutritious, and easy to keep: olive oil, balsamic vinegar, red wine vinegar, dried fruit, figs, dates, olives, apricots, raisins, nuts, hummus, hard cheeses, sourdough bread, sesame crackers, saltine crackers, dried soybeans, jerky, nearly all fresh fruits and vegetables, citrus, oats, granola, cereal, salt, pepper, and meat jerky.

One of the sweetest perks to traveling around and then hiking or walking a few miles exploring the immediate area is that you get in better shape. People underestimate just how sedentary their lives have become. Vanaboding will help keep you leaner and happier without paying for a gym membership. Why struggle on a treadmill in a sweaty smelly gym with a hundred other fat sick people when you could be hiking a secluded meadow with beautiful peaceful plants and animals as companions?

Sleeping and Parking

If you follow my advice when choosing your van to use for Vanaboding you will never have to spend money on campgrounds or hotels. This element is deceptively simple, but it saves you thousands of dollars a year. It saves you countless hours wasted because you can avoid the whole check in and check out process. It makes it possible to add *many* hours a day to every single day of your trip. How? Because you can stay where you want to stay without worrying about leaving and traveling 50 miles away to a hotel you have a reservation at. You don't have to cut your activities short to find, travel to, and check in to some hotel or campground. When you stay in hotels you have to call ahead and make firm reservations and keep them. When Vanaboding you don't have to plan ahead at all or even think about where you will spend the night if you don't want to.

We typically stay in a hotel or campground once or twice every 30 days while on the road just for a change of pace. If you only do it once in a while it doesn't cut into your budget too much. Then we enjoy a normal hot shower or bath, watch some television, swim in the pool, do laundry and catch up on Internet work.

Some people worry about sleeping somewhere out of the ordinary like beside a secluded lake, or at the foot of a mountain overlooking the sea. People are so accustomed to sleeping in the same place every night in the same house they think it is bizarre, or scary, or even unsafe. Don't worry. We have camped this way thousands of nights over the last 20 years. We have been awakened by a disturbance only three times in all those years. I repeat, only *three times out of thousands!*

Once when in a parking lot surrounding San Francisco's Palace of Fine Arts, we were awakened by some teenagers walking by after a concert at 3 am. One of them tapped the side of the van with their hand. They were just being kids and didn't do anything but frighten us awake. Twice while parking overnight in California's public parks the police came by, politely knocked on the van door, shined the flashlight in and asked "what are you doing here?" and "sir show me your driver's license."

After satisfying themselves that we were not up to anything illegal they politely cited the law in that particular part of California that prohibits you from sleeping in a vehicle overnight in a public park. They asked us to move. Then they left stating they will come back before the night is over to make sure we are gone. We get up, drive to another spot *outside* the park area and go right back to sleep. No big deal. No harm done. Frankly I am glad the police are patrolling. I consider this a blessing not a nuisance.

Since 1993 we have *never* been ticketed or asked to step out of our van. Note though, we *never have open alcoholic containers in the van*. When we drink a bottle of wine with our sunset dinner we do so outside the van, finish the bottle, and do not recork it. We do not put it back in the cooler. Even though the van is now your abode, or temporary house, it is still considered a passenger vehicle. An open alcohol container in a motor vehicle is bad news in every state.

The first few times you sleep out somewhere new you will feel strange. At first my wife and I would just lay there for hours listening to every sound and our imaginations would create all sorts of wild ideas. After a few weeks we realized that nothing bad was going to happen. There was nothing going on outside our van that needed our attention.

Think about it. All over the country thousands of people are sleeping in tiny cloth tents in wild wilderness areas filled with bears, mountain lions, snakes, and strangers. Hundreds of thousands of people are homeless and sleep unprotected and exposed outside with nothing more than a blanket. While Vanaboding we have a permanent nearly hurricane proof steel house (abode) around us all night long. Now, locked up and secure inside our white cabin we sleep without a care in the world. You will too if you follow my instructions for choosing the right parking spot, security plan, and van layout.

Many times my wife and I are so busy goofing off hiking, mall shopping, or visiting good restaurants, museums, and art galleries during the day that we don't really know where we will spend the night yet. It can actually be part of the adventure. Let it go. Enjoy the day. Later you may find yourself catching a great dinner and movie then heading to a bookstore to relax from nine to midnight. Sometimes, if our options look limited we may drive around for 10 minutes earlier in the day, and pick out where we will spend the night. Then we go about our day, come back at bedtime, and get some shuteye.

Wait until it gets dark to pull in and park for the night in populated areas, that way you are not tempted to sit up and do things that will reveal you are staying in the van. Park, douse the lights immediately, put up the windshield cover black side facing out, and go to bed. Do not go in or out of the van, turn the lights or radio on, or draw any attention to yourself. We normally lie there recuperating for the first 20 minutes talking and laughing *quietly* about the day, discussing the next day's plans and then drift off to sleep. Obviously when camping in the wilderness you can stay up as late as you want and make as much noise as you want.

One of my readers pointed out that they had been approached by security a few times over the years when they were sleeping in mall parking lots because they snored so loudly they could be heard 50 feet away. She wanted to know what I suggested she do about it. I thought it was hilarious, and I honestly could not provide a suitable answer other than to say she needs to find a place to sleep where stealth is not necessary.

See the BOOK portion of Money Saving Resources (http://www.vanabode.com/camp/amazon-travel-store.htm) on the Internet for books that list, map, and provide directions to: thousands of places to legally park free overnight. Great choices for parking in the city with the best ones listed first are: 1) any 24 hour business like a Wal-Mart, casino, nightclub, hotel or restaurant; as long as you realize there will be some noise and activity through the night. 2) Curbside in any nice looking neighborhood. This works great because neighbor "A" thinks you are visiting neighbor "B" and neighbor "B" thinks you are visiting neighbor "A" or most times neither of them care. 3) Churches, libraries, hospitals, and small business parking lots that are off the main street. 4) Rest areas, repair shops where anyone driving by thinks your vehicle is being worked on the next day.

You can park anywhere that meets the following criteria: It should be safe, as quiet as needed to get a good night's sleep, and oriented so you can pull straight out should the need arise. Park where a clean plain van with dark tinted windows parked overnight will not draw attention. In front of a bank, for instance, is not a good choice. We once stayed for 3 nights in a Sears's parking lot right beside all the Sears appliance repair vans. Our van looked just like the repair vans and we were never bothered.

Some Vanaboders like to put a "for sale" sign on the windshield before going to sleep in a public parking lot. If you do this make sure you know that the owners of the lot are gone for the night and will not call for your van to be towed. Realize that although the sign is clever, and will normally keep the police away, it also invites people to stop by and check out the van. They may be kicking the tires and looking in the windows while you are trying to sleep. I don't recommend this method.

It very rarely ever happens, but if you are ever approached while asleep or in your vehicle use common sense just like you would if you just got groceries and climbed into your car at the local supermarket near your house. If someone calls out to you, shines a light in your vehicle or knocks on the sides of the van, get up, go to the driver's seat, blast the horn and immediately leave. See the **Security** chapter for more on this. If you find the police outside do *not* drive away. Make sure you are *not* holding any kind of weapon either. Remember you have not done anything wrong. Be polite. Don't panic. Don't let one rare uncomfortable incident ruin your holiday. Everything will be fine.

They will ask questions like "what are you doing here?" Just say "We drove a long way today. We were tired so we parked for a short rest so we would not have an accident. Officer we want to make sure we don't do anything wrong. If sleeping here for a few hours is a problem then we will head up the road towards (wherever you planned on going the next day anyway)." The officer may *know* that you are trying to sleep overnight in a place where others may frown at the practice. But I have never met a policeman that cared. They are simply there to enforce the law and look out for us. They are not there to harass or cause problems for tourists.

Once again we have only had this happen 2 times in 20+ years of sleeping like this thousands of times. Sometimes they will actually *hint* that you can go back to sleep without coming out and saying it. If they say something like "okay I see you were only resting. I don't want you driving tired and dangerously. I am leaving now and will not be patrolling this area again tonight". Then you can rest assured they will leave you alone and don't care if you stay the rest of the night.

Of course we do not stay in the city all the time. There are millions of acres of public lands, state parks, national parks and recreational areas that you can camp, sleep, park, and hang out in all over the United States. We love the outdoors, so most of the time we camp off grid. Small country roads that lead only to a farmhouse or two, country flea market parking lots, small parks that are *not* posted "no overnight parking", lakes, rivers, secluded fields, pastures, and wooded areas are all perfect for Vanabode sleeping a night or two. We have a lot of fun sleeping out in the deserts of New Mexico, Arizona, Utah, California and Nevada because it is so cool and dry at night that we can clearly see innumerable stars.

Casinos still make one of the best places to Vanabode the night away in regardless of what part of the country you are in. They have huge 24-hour parking lots so you will always go unnoticed. The entertainment and fun offered is usually free or very cheap. The food is always worth more than what you pay for it. You can hook to the Internet using their free connection by simply asking for the password at the front desk. It is nice to catch up on some television in the many bars and boutiques too. Casino bathrooms are huge, clean, and well appointed. Security is usually roaming around on golf carts or bicycles and in big cities like Vegas in patrol cars, so safety is not a problem.

In Las Vegas the casinos and related shopping malls and tourist attractions are so nice we stay for a month or longer sometimes rotating between just two casinos. There are a lot more casinos to enjoy in this country than just the ones in Las Vegas. For example, during one of our 30 day trips up the West Coast we stayed nearly every night for free at many different Indian based casinos (like the Seven Cedars Indian Casino in Washington.) Nearly every state has casinos now, so take advantage of this great Vanabode opportunity.

We also van camp all over millions of acres of Bureau of Land Management (BLM) public land for a month or two at a time. Updated resources in the BOOK portion Vanabode travel store (http://www.vanabode.com/camp/amazon-travel-store.htm) list places to camp for two weeks at a time free. After two weeks you must move at least 1 mile away and your 2 week calendar limit starts over. *Many Vanabode camp forever this way.* We always see extraordinary wildlife and nightlife in these wooded off road camping places. I like hearing the mournful cries of the nocturnal animals all night long. The nice thing about camping like this is we don't need to be secretive about our occupancy. Instead we *advertise that we are "home".* This keeps everyone away and gives us privacy. Outsiders assume if we are IN our van camping then we are probably armed, so either for that reason or out of respect for privacy we have *never* been approached while in the great outdoors.

The government BLM land administrators *want* you to legally access and enjoy these government lands; participating in what is called *dispersed camping*, or camping in places other than official campgrounds. However, the private citizens that hold grazing leases, surface water rights or even gold or other precious metal mineral claims, will usually not want you on the property. The private citizens don't want free campers around, even though they are usually not breaking the law. They will often lie to you and tell you that you are trespassing.

If you plan on doing a lot of deep BLM land camping, and find that you are running into these folks that want to control what is not theirs, use your cell phone's GPS system to determine exactly where you are. Then use the BLM surface rights map (you can get these online or from the local BLM office) to show who "owns" what, and who has what rights. For example you might find the guy trying to move you along has rights to let his cattle graze *on* the BLM land you are camping on, but that the land is NOT private. It is owned by the taxpayers and managed by the United States government for the enjoyment of us all.

I have never personally had anyone ask me to move on, probably because there are just too many millions of acres of land to choose from that we hardly even see anybody. If you are confronted make casual, pleasant conversation rather than be confrontational. Let them know how long you plan on staying, that you will clean up after yourself, that you will not be digging up the ground or polluting the local water. Be respectful. Follow all local customs.

Here in the remote areas we lay on the bed with the back doors open staring at everything: the glorious views of the countryside, the tree filled forests, the rivers, the sunsets, the sunrises, and the star-studded pitch-black night skies. Enjoy yourself by getting a good night's sleep, because with plenty of rest, you can do just about anything with vigor.

When camping in the wilderness remember it is sometimes as much as 15-20 degrees cooler amongst the trees, than it is out in the open. Trees give shade but they also breathe and transpire water making it substantially cooler among them. It is also much cooler at higher elevations, so when you want more warmth drive down. When you want cooler temperatures, drive up.

Here's how bad things can happen to you when you do not get enough sleep. My wife Kelly and I were visiting some of her family in Georgia. I walked back from the pool alone to her Uncle Julian and Aunt Myra's house where we were staying for a few days. I walked in the front door, shut and locked it behind me, left my shoes just inside, and yelled to Myra and Kelly jokingly, "Honey, I'm Home!"

As I walked through the living room and glanced upstairs to the second floor and then back to the kitchen I got a strange feeling. I walked into the kitchen and yelled again "Honey, I'm home!" No answer. I guessed Kelly and Myra had walked down to the basement to tend to our bunny Bugsy. As I turned to go back into the living room a strange warmth came over me, I began to sweat almost immediately and my heart began to race. I felt distant and dream like. Nothing made sense. My mind raced and I thought; where are they? What is going on?

I was scared and could not figure out why. I felt like a ghost was watching me. Then I saw it. An aquarium filled with small fish that were swimming frantically around and around. I saw things thrown on the floor that I didn't remember being there. I felt something watching me. I turned the corner on my way back to the front door (they have a HUGE house) and the hair on the back of my neck stood up. My hands began to shake. Adrenaline shot through me. Then I saw it; a cold black cat frozen stiffly mid-launch in the armchair by the door. His eyes were brilliant yellow, completely dilated and wide open as if by a really bad taxidermist. He was as terrified as I was.

It was in that instant that I realized Myra and Julian did not have a cat. They did not have an aquarium. I was not in Julian and Myra's house. I was so tired I had went into the house next door to the one I was supposed to go in. I *slowly* passed the cat, then lurched forward, fumbled with the lock, opened the door, and was halfway through it when I had to reach back in to grab my shoes. I stumbled down the walkway and onto the sidewalk, threw my shoes on and ran *next door* to Julian and Myra's house. I begged Myra not to accept any phone calls, in case the neighbor called the police. Myra laughed so hard she almost face planted her blueberries and milk. Kelly and Julian were hysterical. My heart was beating real hard.

When I calmed down I thought "What if there had been a big guard dog in that house, or someone undressed, or a man with a gun? I could have been eaten or shot and killed just because I was sleep deprived." While traveling sleep good, worse could happen.

Personal Hygiene

Using the bathroom, bathing, and cleaning up is one of the most important topics to address when traveling long term. Good personal hygiene is very important when interacting successfully with people while on the road and maintaining a positive mental state. Many people go tent camping and they get this nagging feeling 2 days into the trip..."*I need to hurry and get back home.*" They don't realize where that feeling comes from. Later they say something like "*camping is just not for me.*"

This keeps them from relaxing and enjoying *where they are right now.* They find that they are not *present.* Why? Because on a subconscious level they are simply not happy with the condition of their *body.* They have let their personal hygiene suffer and that underlying feeling is pushing them to get home so they can fix it. They do not understand that they were uncomfortable because they were not at peace with their body. They were not relaxed, comfortable, and clean. Don't make this mistake when traveling.

Take it slow. It is very important to feel like yourself while trying exciting new things. However, don't think for one minute that the joy of hiking to the top of that extraordinary mountain is going to completely replace the *Essentials of a Great Life.* If you come back down that evening, go to bed dirty, tired and hungry, it will become a very short trip fast. Regardless of how many fun, exciting, and romantic activities you do, you will still need to maintain a good grasp on these principles: *excellent food, great sleep, good personal hygiene, healthy sex, and protection from the elements.* If you skimp on these you will feel distant and out of place. This will lead to disappointment and stress. This is why you hear so many people say they don't like camping.

Neglect personal hygiene and it will always ruin your journey. For example, when staying in our *house* we shower every day, sometimes twice a day. But how do you do bathe when Vanaboding? How do you brush or floss your teeth, shave, clean up after using the bathroom, wash your hands, put on makeup, wash and dry your hair, do your nails, etc.? First I will address the *facilities* that are best for maintaining good hygiene and then I will cover each of the individual hygienic *tasks.* Choose the solution you prefer for the situation you find yourself in and ignore the rest.

Single User Bathrooms can be found at convenience stores, fast food restaurants, small restaurants, gas stations, etc. They are setup for one person at a time, have a lock on the door, and usually have everything you need to take a hot sponge bath, shave, use the toilet, sanitize, floss and brush your teeth, and get a good look at your face in the mirror. If a key is required for admittance let the female in your group ask for the key. Then the two of you can go in together. This way you don't tie up both bathrooms or draw a suspicious and nosey audience. It also makes you feel safer since occasionally someone will bang on the door for admittance.

Multiple User Bathrooms can be found at department stores and restaurants. These type bathrooms are my least favorite. They are designed for more than one person at a time and so they usually do not have a lock on the door. Therefore you have no privacy. Management, employees, custodians, and other patrons can come in at any time. If you are a hardy soul there is nothing to fear. When somebody walks in and you are standing there washing your hair in the sink, well too bad. Management cannot actually do anything but ask you to leave. By then you are finished and ready to leave anyway. I do not like the idea of any kind of confrontation so I rarely use multiple use bathrooms for conducting personal hygiene other than simple wash ups and toilet usage.

Truck Stops can be found nearly every 25 miles on nearly every major interstate highway or state highway in the country. They are my wife's favorite method of clean up. Truck drivers sleep in the back of the truck cab each night while out driving the country for months at a time. Therefore they need a hot shower each night without paying for a hotel room. So, most all the fuel stations that accept tractor-trailers install private full service bathrooms with showers. The male in the group simply goes up to the counter, and asks for a shower pass. Do not advertise that you are *not* driving a big rig tractor-trailer. If they ask for your truck number, simply answer "I don't need that on the receipt". Or you can simply make one up "truck number 675" They will sell you the use of a nice big private bathroom complete with towels, wash cloths, toilet, shower, mirrors, and sink for about $4 to $8. My wife and I share the one shower and bathroom pass and go in together.

Gym or Health Clubs are best used for longer stays in one area. For instance, when we stay in the heart of San Francisco for a month or longer at a time we don't want to worry about cleaning up every day. So we purchase a one-month YMCA membership giving us use of the gym, free parking, fitness classes, showers, pools, and a place to catch the evening news, charge up our computers, and more. On the application we use a local address that we just picked out of the phone book *before* going in to apply. If you plan on being in one area for less than a week be careful. You do not want them to know that you will not be buying the annual membership. Just tell them you will *consider* purchasing the annual membership. Simply request the 1-7 day free trial memberships that most health clubs offer using any local address that you picked out of the phone book. Do not tell them you are traveling through in your van. This way it's free. When you're done a few days later you simply leave, fresh, clean and without expense or obligation.

Campgrounds can be found nearly everywhere except in highly congested areas of states like California and cities like San Francisco and New York City. You can pay to camp there for the night and use the shower, pool, laundry facilities, Internet access, bathroom, and clubhouse like the other campers. In many cases you can skip the cost though and simply drive in and around the campground until you find the shower facilities. Many campgrounds have pay showers where you drop in a quarter for every 5 minutes. This is my favorite method of showering in civilization.

Van baths are not as big a deal as they seem. If you are absolutely disgusting and want to stand in a hot shower for 15 minutes then obviously you cannot bathe in the van. However that is rarely the case. I prefer bathing in the van nearly 90% of the time because of its simplicity, and complete privacy. I don't have to carry anything anywhere. I don't have to find a public bathroom or wonder what anyone thinks. I simply pull out one of the plastic storage tubs or my biggest cooler, empty a little water into it, step inside and wash with soap and water. Then I use a spray bottle with clean water to rinse, step out, dry off, and empty the dirty water outside the van. I am done in 5-7 minutes and I feel refreshed. Sometimes I use the 12-volt mini oven discussed elsewhere in this book to heat up 8 to 10 ounces of water and sponge bathe off. Problem solved. It is not glamorous, nor is it comfortable since I can't stand up in my van, but it is fast, cheap, easy and requires nearly no equipment.

Homemade Shower - you can take a hand pressurized pump, garden spray bottle that typically holds from 1 to 2 gallons of water, spray paint it black, sit it in the sun, and within

2 hours it will be warm enough to give you hot water to bathe or shower with. If you are in a hurry, set up some aluminum reflective panels around the water bottle to magnify the sun. You can also heat up smaller quantities of water using the solar oven discussed in the **Food** chapter, or by sitting black painted jugs on the dash of your van in the sun.

Public Facilities that may include private bathroom stalls, sinks, showers, internet access, and more can be found at beach pavilions, public parks, libraries, health clinics, hospitals, convention halls, hotel lobbies and outdoor pool areas, casinos, or any other large organized high traffic facility. Usually there are so many people using these type facilities that you will not get any attention at all. This of course is what you want. Go in, smile, find the bathroom without asking for help, then clean up and leave. These places will rarely have single user bathrooms so if privacy is of importance use one of my other suggestions.

Now for the actual *acts* of personal hygiene. Bathing this way takes getting used to. But it is worth it. Keep clean and refreshed so you feel good about the trip rather skimping and killing the fun. Besides, do you really want to scare the guy at the counter when you first walk into the store unshaven, hair askew, with a dried peanut shell on your upper lip, smelling like a homeless sleep under the bridge dude?

Water supply, plumbing, sanitation, and sewage collection and disposal have been among the top logistical challenges since the dawn of civilization. Only in the past 200 years has it become so incredibly easy to defecate indoors and have it miraculously swished away. For most of the world, even day, there is no flush toilet or inside hot water source for showers. Don't fret. We stay very clean and wash up every day while traveling. So can you.

Feeling clean and feeling at home in your own skin is very important, so be prepared. Take the time to visit single use bathrooms where you can lock the door and use the sink and toilet privately. Take your reduced travel size shaving creams, soaps, and shampoos in and work your magic using the supplied paper towels or the blow dryer to finish up. Sponge baths, hot water shaves, quick shampoos, makeup applications, teeth brushing, flossing, nail clipping, are all easily done in most restrooms.

Bathing, simple wash-ups - If you are in a populated area it is fast and easy to simply sit in or lean over one of the plastic clothes tubs shown in the **Inventory** chapter and bathe right in the van. Drain a little water from the cooler into the tub, saving a water bottle or two for the final rinse, and then sponge bathe off. You can get very clean this way though the water is cold sometimes. It sounds primitive but it is quite refreshing and it works. It is also free, fast and easy.

Of course if you are in a remote area where privacy is not an issue you can use an outdoor method like a solar shower, or a hot bath in an inflatable baby pool or plastic storage tub. Heat the water by placing dark colored or painted plastic jugs in the sun for two hours either outside your van or on the dash. You can also heat water by using any electric thermos or cooking device that runs off of your 12-volt system in the van, by using your solar oven, or by using the single flame blowtorch used for cooking.

Recently we invested in an instant hot water device since we plan on staying in some colder climates next year. The instant system heats the water using the same fuel used in our small one burner propane stove. This eliminates having to keep up with 2 different kinds of fuel. This ZODI brand is highly recommended, as it is of super high quality and well designed.

I also like the fact that everything you see in the picture relating to the heater fits nicely *into* the carrying case. In the picture the carrying case has a black trash bag in it and is being used as the water source. Look closely and you will see that there is adequate water flow in a good pattern from the built in showerhead. Within 3 seconds of igniting the propane using the built in push button ignition system (no lighter or matches needed) the water is flowing out warm. Within 6 seconds it is super-hot. I think this system represents a near perfect, inexpensive, easy way to have hot showers and baths anytime you want, nearly anywhere.

Remember as explained elsewhere in this book the burning of propane creates the same carbon monoxide that burning other fuels does. It can kill you. Never burn propane or any other fuel inside the van. Use it outdoors only since it can cause an explosion. The words "ONLY USE OUTDOORS" is printed right on the unit. Carbon monoxide is odorless and colorless. Do not take chances with it inside your van.

The pump runs on four D size batteries. You will get about 50 gallons of heating use between battery and propane changes. The super heavy duty carrying case doubles as your water reservoir holding up to 4 gallons of water at a time. You could put the pump in any water source though, be it cooler, bucket, pond, stream, sink, baby pool, etc. My picture shows what I do. I place a watertight trash bag in the carrying case that comes with the device. Then I put 4 gallons of water in there, drop the sealed pump in the water, ignite the flame, and take my shower. The entire setup takes about 2 minutes.

I noticed it lights *much* faster if you turn the gas on very low, barely on, then push the igniter button 4-5 times real fast. Once lit you can turn up the heat by turning on the gas more. Having the gas setting low initially not only helps it ignite better but also prevents the release of too much unburned propane which could lead to a flare up. Once lit, adjusting the gas setting to high makes the water heat faster and helps guard against high winds blowing out the flame.

You can purchase one of these instant-on-demand hot water heaters at most camping stores, at Wal-Mart during the right season, or from the links on Camping Resources (http://www.vanabode.com/camp/links.htm). Visit Zodi.com to see other options and buy right from them if you wish. They also sell quick setup outdoor shower curtain contraptions for privacy showering outdoors. You can also shower in your swimsuit if people are around. Sometimes we set up the unit outside, heat up 5 gallons of water, and then take the water into the van and bathe off.

Do not let this be a bigger issue than it has to be. If you need this unit and you will take the time to use it then buy one. They cost from $82 (like mine) to $210 depending on how big of a unit you want. Otherwise just use my other strategies. I purchased the unit mainly to test it for my customers and it works great. I mostly use it in cold weather and I don't use it for most of my showering.

When using a facility that has a hot air blow dryer for drying your hands you can use the same machine to dry your freshly shampooed hair. Simply rotate the valve up instead of down. You can also use these air dryers to dry your washcloth, sponge, toothbrush and anything else that got wet during your clean up session.

When using public facilities it is best to carry the miniature-sized containers of toothpaste, deodorant, shampoo, soap, etc., in with you in such a way that nobody can see them. My wife just uses her purse. I throw on my lightweight fisherman's vest that has more than 20 pockets. I keep it stocked with all the toiletries so at a moment's notice I can throw it on, walk in, clean up, and leave without arousing any curiosity.

Toilet duties present some people with more problems than most other personal hygiene related issues. We have not had anything happen that we could not easily overcome. We purchased the portable toilet we are currently using over 7 years ago and it has worked flawlessly for us ever since. You can see a picture of it in the **Inventory** chapter. My wife even prefers to use this portable toilet when we are in our hometown, rather than use the toilet in a public restaurant or department store. It all started one time when we were about to go into a big shopping mall and she went to the back of the van, pulled the curtain, urinated, and said "why would anyone want to own a car when they can do this in a van?" I laughed so hard I got the collar of my shirt wet.

After sitting down and urinating in the toilet we use the spray bottle to spray it all down, flush it, and spray a second time on the inside rim so a little clean water stays in the bowl. There is no smell. At first we used a blue colored portable toilet sanitizer like that used in big motorhome toilets. However, it spilled in the van one time and created toxic fumes. Our eyes were watering and it took hours to get it all out. NEVER use chemicals in your portable toilet I don't care what the manufacturer says. We prefer to just use water. It is cleaner. It has no bad smell. It has no toxic elements. It is free.

After about a week of urination by the both of us the toilet is full. The portable toilet I recommend detaches from the seat and you can easily carry the storage chamber portion *only* into a bathroom or wooded area to dump it. See photo in the **Inventory** chapter. We usually time this activity with a truck stop shower, hotel stay, or campground visit so that we can spend some time *showering off* the toilet itself and giving it a thorough cleaning. We have never had a problem with smells, leaks, or good sanitary conditions using these strategies.

Defecation presents a different set of troubles. Even though the portable toilet can accept solid waste we prefer to not defecate in it. We are worried that the smell and clean up procedure would be too nasty or unsanitary. Instead we try to do all defecation in public bathrooms, at stores, campgrounds, or when we are out hiking and have no choice, in the wilderness.

Occasionally one of us wakes up in the middle of the night and has to go. For safety reasons I normally insist that we do not go outside at night. In these rare cases we will put a small garbage bag over the toilet seat, and down into it, essentially lining the toilet with the bag. Then we do our business, tie the bag up tight and put this bag into yet another bag and seal it up as well. Then we dispose of the bagged waste the next morning as soon as we can find an appropriate receptacle.

When defecating use toilet paper first then baby wipes. These can be carried easily in a backpack when hiking. You can make your own unscented wipes. Take paper towels or napkins and fold them to fit into baby wipe dispenser. Then soak them with water. If you want a better cleaner simply squeeze a little lemon or lime juice in with the water. Do not use them to clean your face with though since your eyes may burn from the citrus.

Baby wipes or moist paper towels, spray bottles, and plenty of toilet paper allow for a completely clean area when you are done. Do not skimp or you will feel dirty all day. Clean thoroughly to prevent any negative health issues. Take the time to do it right.

Some people fret about dropping a garbage bag containing feces into a garbage can. I don't. Every day millions of city dwellers drop millions of bags of dirty diapers and smelly pooch pack burritos containing dog feces into personal and public garbage cans. The little bit we travelers contribute is not even a drop in the bucket compared to this.

Hair Care affects some more than others. If you have short hair there is nothing to do differently. If you have long hair and are planning on camping and exploring mainly outdoor activities like hiking, swimming, boating, hunting, photography, or mountain climbing you might consider cutting your hair short. This will minimize the time, money and effort you have to spend taking care of it. This also makes it less likely that ticks or other invasive insects will attach themselves to your head, neck or creep inside your ears undetected.

I keep my hair very long because I like the protection from the sun. I have had skin cancer removed from my face (http://www.vanabode.com/camping-sun-protection.htm) more than once so this is of priority to me. Click the link to see pictures but be **WARNED** they are gruesome! My wife has very long hair too. If she cannot easily wash it daily she will sometimes braid it into one long ponytail. Her hair can look good for days this way. We sleep almost exclusively in the van so we worry less about invasive insects than those camping in tents on the ground.

Nails are more important when doing a lot of outdoor activities than they are in the typical stay at home and go to work lifestyle. Obviously, you may not be worried about them being completely beautiful when out white water rafting or camping. However, if they are not properly trimmed, cleaned and kept dry they can become a problem. Never trim either your fingernails or toenails very short right before any new outdoor activity. The longer nails will prevent your finger and toes from being tender, blistered, or damaged from doing what seems like the simplest of tasks. Rowing a boat, hiking in new specialty boots, scrambling over some medium size rocks, accidentally stubbing your toe, or kicking a rock will be a lot easier to take with longer nails.

When hiking always stop every hour and remove your shoes and socks. Let everything dry out for 3-5 minutes. Remove every single grain of sand from your shoes and socks. Doing this helps prevent toe rot, tender toes, blisters, and infections that can ruin your walking experience for days. Whenever it is safe to do so wear open sandals that allow your feet to remain completely dry. Immediately began using a disinfectant spray on your feet and toes if you see any weird discoloration around the toenails.

Dental Care including flossing and brushing your teeth presents no special problems while traveling. Use clean water and keep your toothbrush dry and clean between brushings. Do not use the water from any unsanitary source such as a river or lake. Bacteria there can enter your digestive system and wreak havoc for days, months and even years.

Shaving can present problems for some people. I simply modify my behavior from shaving every day to shaving once a week. Unless I am attending a nice upscale event nobody really cares if I am a little unshaven. Not being forced to shave daily represents one more way that Vanaboding gives me some time in my life back. It is just one more task that is not always necessary due to this lifestyle, so I skip it. If you want to shave daily just like you do in your house then you can carry your toiletries into the facilities described above and carry on. Except for the multi user bathrooms nobody will even know. If you are shaving from the van, purchase an electric razor and recharge it using the *inverter* shown in the **Inventory** chapter. Then you won't even need water.

Makeup is important to many people, especially women. I know some that are not comfortable in public without it. They won't even face me for a casual conversation without it. Makeup is good for sun damage prevention especially for those outside a lot like we are. It can be very helpful for preventing damage to your lips. Whatever the reason, putting on makeup simply requires having a good steady mirror and decent lighting.

Making some tasks easier. Set dark colored jugs or black painted milk jugs in the sun to heat water. Be careful the water can get *very* hot on sunny days. Use a spray bottle to shower off with, get debris out of your eyes, cool off, and clean up after nasty bathroom breaks. Hang a simple solar hot shower device outside on top of the van before going on a hike. It is essentially a black bag filled with water attached to a short rubber hose with a shut off handle. By the time you get back the water is hot and the shower is very welcoming. You can buy this from the specialty stores like Camping World shown in Camping Resources (http://www.vanabode.com/camp/links.htm).

Inflate a portable baby pool, put some water in it, set it outside the van, and put a black piece of plastic over it before leaving for a hike. When you get back you can jump right in the warm fresh water to bathe off. If you get overheated, wet a shirt, put it on, and stand in front of a fan to cool down fast.

Liquid vitamin E can be carried in the van and with you in your pocket when hiking. It is fantastic as a makeup remover, works perfectly as a personal lubricant, and prevents chapped and blistered lips. It has little to no taste. It is a great skin moisturizer because the body absorbs it more easily than cream lotions. It also speeds the healing of some topical skin rashes, sunburns, or itchy patches of skin. Purchase the *thin* liquid vitamin E not the thick kind. When you turn the bottle upside down the bubble of air should rise to the top nearly instantly. Most stores like Walgreen's, CVS, and Eckerd's Drugs carry it.

Sex

Some people put their sex lives on hold when camping. They leave home for a week and because they are out of their element they stop enjoying their bodies. This is a mistake. The definition of *romance* is: "a quality or feeling of mystery, excitement, and remoteness from everyday life". The very best time to enjoy some fresh fulfilling love is when you are out of your element: this *"remoteness from everyday life" is the very essence of Vanaboding.* A healthy sex life during the appropriate portion of one's life is important to ones being whole, complete, and satisfied. I'm not talking about a 2-minute quickie behind a strand of dusty bushes off some dirt road. Instead take the time to offer each other the very best, fun, adventurous, amorous love you can.

Have fun in interesting places, not populated ones. Many women are more concerned with "being exposed or getting caught outdoors" than men are. So men you should take this into consideration if you want to indulge. Plan to get further away from others who may be out hiking or exploring so your spouse will be more comfortable. Outdoor sex can be so much fun because most people rarely do it. When was the last time you laid down on a soft blanket in the deep woods, embraced by the sounds and smells of the forest, or prairie, or mountain, or valley or beach, and made slow passionate love? Get your Adam and Eve on!

My wife and I hiked up a small hill above thousands of motorcycle enthusiasts at the world's largest biker rally in Sturgis (http://www.rvforsaleguide.com/sturgis-motorcycle-pictures.htm). We got to the top and looked back at a valley full of thousands of screaming bikers, parties, campsites, tents, motorhomes, races, and portable pool parties. It was fun but noisy. Then we turned and looked the other way at the most gorgeous valley of wild flowers and a prairie full of herds of grazing sheep. The little lambs were in their own world jumping and kicking about, completely oblivious to us at the top of the hill.

We descended into the prairie as the sun set, and the herds of sheep parted like water, some flowed uphill, and some moved left, some right. We climbed atop a giant earthmover tractor and lay side by side on the huge hood. The sheep called to each other. The wind whispered through the incredibly tall grass. In the distance Bison snorted and rolled on the golden plains. The place, the moment, still to this day suspended in time, allowed us to leave everything but each other behind. We made love under the stars and then fell asleep. We woke up about midnight, and for fear we might roll over wrong and fall 10 feet to the ground, we hiked back to our campsite. Based from our Vanabode it was an easy to accomplish romantic evening, but utterly unforgettable.

One time in Florida we climbed up into a lifeguard stand 12 feet off the ground and made out under the full moon. Waves were crashing all around us. To this day I can still hear the gentle hiss of the bubbles collapsing as the water receded. The air was salty and cool. The sand and our bodies glowed neon under the full moon.

We once went nuts on the seat of a jet ski in the full sun. We were floating ten feet from the sandy shore in Lake Powell Utah, where some of the most incredible cliffs and rock formations plunge into the cool impossibly blue waters. It was fantastic, adventurous and very memorable. I laugh whenever I think of the old saying: Make love not war, it sounds so corny and over simplistic. Truth is that way sometimes.

I have hundreds of fun stories like these but obviously this is not a romance novel so I will leave it at that. You get the idea. When you are out in strange and interesting surroundings do something wonderful while you are there. Love your lover. Be a friend. Be kind. Hold each other close. Pull the hair from her eyes and tuck it behind her ears. Hold her close when she's cold. Ask her quietly what she thinks of the day, the view, the sky, the night, the future. Grab his hand, squeeze and say "I love you, do you want to....?" Kiss him full on the mouth and linger for a bit. Don't rush. Remember where you are. Think about what you are doing and relish the moment. Be deliberate. Be present!

It is so easy to be good to each other while Vanaboding because all the elements for an incredible romance are in place. You are together and happy. Why? Because if you are following my advice concerning the *Essentials of a Great Life*, you are clean, eating good, sleeping good, having fun, and living as hassle free as one can in this world.

On the practical side, I recommend carrying a small bottle of liquid vitamin E for lubrication and a small ten-serving size container of baby wipes for cleanup. These don't take up much room in a backpack or pocket, are light, and can be used for activities other than sex. As mentioned before liquid vitamin E is great for your face and chapped lips and will keep your skin healthy wherever it is applied. This is especially important if you are camping in a dry desert environment. It has almost no taste so it doesn't introduce a bad taste in your mouth like most lip balms and chap sticks do.

I offer you one of many Biblical passages about outdoor love from the *Song of Solomon Chapter 7 verse 6-13*
"How beautiful you are and how pleasing, O love, with your delights! Your stature is like that of the palm, and your breasts like clusters of fruit. I said, "I will climb the palm tree; I will take hold of its fruit." May your breasts be like the clusters of the vine, the fragrance of your breath like apples, and your mouth like the best wine. May the wine go straight to my lover, flowing gently over lips and teeth. I belong to my lover, and his desire is for me. Come, my lover, let us go to the countryside, and let us spend the night in the villages. Let us go early to the vineyards to see if the vines have budded, if their blossoms have opened, and if the pomegranates are in bloom, there I will give you my love. The mandrakes send out their fragrance, and at our door is every delicacy, both new and old, that I have stored up for you, my lover."

If you have no sex life to speak of before you start serious traveling, then you can continue as you are, if you are both satisfied. Don't force yourself into an uncomfortable situation. However you could use this most romantic of journeys to rekindle the fun. Love like this helps bring people together regardless of past mistakes or disappointments.

Many people think sex when out camping is not worth the time and effort. Some think it's dirty, naughty, or sinful. Wrong! God made our bodies. Enjoy them. Love each other. Make memories that will last forever. When you give of yourself completely nobody can ever take that away from you. Regardless of what the future brings, you can always look back and say "I loved you completely, I did that, I loved you with everything I had. At least I did that part right".

My attempt at romantic poetry while *inspired* on one of our longer Utah trips where we spent some time river rafting goes like this - **Love Boat** *by Jason Odom*

Begin oh so calm and quite, gentle wet kisses lap smooth sides,
then rhythmic rocking, sliding, hips bouncing gently over roundness beneath,
intensity increases, twisting, faster, aft, thrashing to and fro,

out of sync, faster, over, under, back and forth,
stiff flexed muscles bang against stone bones,
plunging under in and out, waves crashing and spinning
pleasure spills overhead, awash in wet delightful squeals,
stroke harder, deeper, trying to guide the craft,
nearly overcome with sweaty waters, muscles tensed like springs,
backs arched and pulling, love mates explode out over the edge,
water falls peeling away beneath, earth far below, floating Wylie coyote style,
suspended in heaven, one minute of eternity passes,
roll over and rest, drift down to the earth,
a mile or two or three beneath us. . .

Protection from the Elements

Protection from the elements may be the easiest to understand of the five Essentials of a Great Life. It is what initially drove people to build houses once they parked the horse drawn prairie wagon. Here's where the mistakes start. Everyone needs a place to abide when there is a hurricane, a tornado, a tsunami, an earthquake, a fire, a torrential downpour, excessive heat, or freezing cold. Plus most want a place to store their possessions. Might as well sleep there too while we are at it right? Each person then chooses a different solution.

When foreigners to the United States were asked "what is the biggest difference between where you are from and how people live in the U.S., they answered; "the size of the houses people in America live in". They were astonished to find that the houses were huge; not out of necessity, but rather as a sign to the public of a person's financial achievement. This is ludicrous. Any time you try to control more of the world than you need to, you give up your most precious resource, your time.

Most choose more house than they can afford and drastically underestimate the *total cost of ownership* (discussed in greater detail in the **Jason's Terms** chapter). Houses cost a lot. Houses require a huge maintenance budget. So you get a huge mortgage from a bank and end up paying three to four times the original cost of the house over the course of some 30 years of payments.

Because you do not own the house yet, you must pay super high insurance rates to "protect the banks investment", and often must buy Private Mortgage Insurance which also "protects the bank" against you defaulting on the loan. Add to those costs the expense of ever increasing real estate taxes, homeowner association dues, utility bills, repair bills, insurance premiums, and running costs like yard care and pest control, and it becomes clear that the *total cost of ownership* is much higher than you anticipated.

So what do you do about it? Most people burn the first 20-25 years of their life attending school with the impression that upon graduation they will be able to acquire a job that will pay them enough to afford all this. Some marry so that the costs associated with this kind of life are shared between two incomes. It is a classic example of one of the worst big picture mistakes people make. Work to buy then die.

People often wrap their entire life around the acquisition of a dry wall box to sleep in. They marry prematurely, burn years of their life in school studying subjects they are not interested in, and spend tons of money paying for it. Then most people find they cannot leave the immediate area except for a pitiful 1 to 2 weeks a year once they *get permission* from their boss to take a vacation. Their entire *world* becomes the house they won't pay off until they are 55 years old. Unhappiness, indebtedness and outright slavery to their jobs become the norm. Once disillusioned, people argue, blame each other and get divorced.

Your job is to work like a hamster on a wheel, then spend your earnings on junk you don't need. As long as the economy is growing (meaning more and more people are spending more and more of their life earnings on stuff) then the big corporate greedy system survives. This is the sickest pyramid scheme of them all. "By working faithfully 8 hours per day, you may eventually get to be the boss and work 12 hours a day" said Robert Frost, the great American poet and winner of four Pulitzer Prizes.

Author Michael Bunker in his extraordinary work titled *Surviving Off Off-Grid: Decolonizing the Industrial Mind* states, "The entire consumer society is designed around the idea that if you make things seem easier for people; if you coddle them so that they have no real skills and so that they become unviable outside of the system; if you control every aspect of their lives, and pander to their every lust and desire; you can control their behavior and make them do your bidding. It makes it easier when, like the man with the pigs, what you want for the victim to do is CONSUME. In ancient societies, slaves were needed to do hard physical labor – like building cities, pyramids, obelisks, or temples. Today, slaves are needed to eat, drink, purchase, and consume."

Folks you only have one life. Don't let others enslave you. You can find a link to this great book *Surviving Off Off-Grid* in the BOOK portion of the Vanabode Store. (http://www.vanabode.com/camp/amazon-travel-store.htm). I highly recommend it because there is content and original thought in this book that I have never seen anywhere else.

"I see young men, my townsmen, whose misfortune it is to have inherited farms, houses, barns, cattle, and farming tools; for these are more easily acquired than got rid of. When the farmer has got his house, he may not be the richer but the poorer for it, and it be the house that has got him." From *Walden* by Henry David Thoreau.

If you could remove the element of cost, there may be little doubt that a well-designed, properly outfitted, heavy duty stationary dwelling is the most *comfortable* place to sleep, bathe, use the bathroom, and eat. However, interestingly enough, static dwellings at any price are *not* the best way to escape the big disasters that can befall mankind.

Houses don't protect you from earthquakes. Most people abandon them and run outside to avoid falling objects or collapsing roofs and walls. Houses can't stop a forest fire; people load their kids in their *minivans* and abandon houses as soon as they see the smoke. Hurricanes tear through roofs and walls and windows and tornadoes make entire communities disappear. How will a house protect you against tsunamis, tidal waves or floods?

There is a better way. Your Vanabode offers the best solution to getting protection against these terrifying elements of nature: *mobility*. I know because I have done it. Later I will recount how we sat through a massive hurricane in Florida in an old motorhome. The best method of all is to simply drive away. Simple but powerful.

Vanabode and you can escape all the disasters that befall the land locked house owner. Just leave! Drive away from hurricanes, earthquakes, tornadoes, floods, and fires. Escape riots, social unrest, bad neighbors, declining property values, persistent messy weather, climate change, local politicians implementing laws and taxes you don't agree with, and more.

This is pure power, freedom, and ultimately the smartest way to live. Obviously the best way to enjoy *protection from the elements* is with a strong, steel Vanabode. It is affordable. It is extremely durable. It is easy to maintain. Most importantly, it is mobile.

Fun

This is important. You *must prioritize your pleasure* in order to have fun because the world is too complicated, and our lives are too busy, to expect fun to take care of itself.

Having fun is one of the most important issues in life. Many marriages end because the fun stops. Relationships of all kinds dry up when life becomes a drag and joy is no longer on the menu. Having fun is especially important while traveling. When you make big sacrifices to be out and about reward yourself. Fortunately, it is easier to have fun while vacationing and enjoying new romantic experiences every day than it is doing virtually anything else. Having fun by *prioritizing your pleasure* is one of the things in life that most people never do, or ever do correctly. Do not skimp here or your travels will be hindered and short lived.

In order to prioritize your pleasure identify what you and your travel partner like to do and then do it. For example: if you would rather spend each morning hiking, regardless of how bad the weather is, then go to bed early, get up early, dress and get on with it. Do not let anything stop you. Otherwise your day will become a directionless drag and you will spend all your time on miscellaneous meaningless activities. This is how to waste your time. This is true of any activity that has preference in your life over other activities.

If the only thing you want to do is travel from one big city to the next exploring the art galleries and museums then do just that. Don't slow down or get sidetracked with national parks crowded with hundreds of kids on spring break. Skip right to planning for what you want and *prioritize your pleasure*. Do what *you* want to do *first*.

Most people put what they *really* want last. Take sex for example. Most couples leave this fun and intensely wonderful activity until both people are too tired, or too hungry, or too dirty from the day's outdoor activities, to give it a chance at being exceptional. If you were looking forward to making love under that big oak tree you saw the night before on your sunset scouting trip, then say so when you first get up. Plan for it. Share your idea with your mate and enjoy yourselves before you do anything else. Then you will be very happy with how the rest of your day goes.

If you love fishing and your mate only wants to hike, then do a little research. Don't lazily avoid each other's needs and desires. Realize that meeting these needs is the foundation of pleasure. Find a secluded lake you have to hike 5 miles to get to. Or find any large lake and hike around it until the hiker is pleased. Then stop and fish until the fisherman has caught his fill. Then you can *both* come back happy. Have Fun! Make a plan that accounts for what each person wants. Execute it.

If you are open to change you can have more fun. You can quickly start doing new fun activities because you are out of your familiar surroundings. Try new things. When out camping you can try new foods. Conversely you could relive activities you forgot you liked. Try waking up at 2 am to go outside and hear whatever wild animals are out. Check out the various seasonal festivals, art shows, conventions, etc. that are running all over the country all year long. Ask yourself "what have I always wanted to do or try" and then do or try it. Pleasure for most people is illusive; but it does not have to be. Make fun a priority instead spending your entire life and all your energy on a job or career you barely like.

"The 9 mile round trip hike through heavy forest was a real treat, except for not being able to walk upright the next day", from our Zion Utah trip in the **Destinations Guide** online.

This comes from my old notes on one of our fun trips to Glacier National Park. *"A tear slid down my cheek. A grown man driving down the road, my wife asleep in the back, and here I am crying. A big truck just passed me with hundreds of chickens jammed in crowded pens. They hunkered down against the wind blowing through the open cages, sending their pretty white feathers backwards. They were so scared on their trip down the highway that they could not figure out which way to face. Many laid eggs. Some eggs rolled back and forth while others lay smashed, yolks dripping down from one cage to another, yellow tears joining mine, dripping down the highway."*

Go where the sights need no binoculars. Go where clean water flows. Go where electricity is not needed because the weather is perfect. Live there as long as you like.

Navigation

In the **Simplify** chapter I explain that the *first* thing you should do when entering every new city or destination is to stop and get directions. Ask how to get from where you are to the most important of places: the tourist information centers. These are run by local agencies staffed by locals that know their stuff. They offer more time saving, valuable free information about *where you are right now* than I could pack into 10 books like this one. Take a full hour if you need to. This is the most important thing you can do to make your trip fantastic, rather than just a tiring headache. Skip this step, and you will burn time doing something unimpressive one place while everyone else is one mile up the road at a mind blowing first class destination point. Without good local information you will stare at the seagull in the grocery store parking lot, while five minutes away others watch a blue heron chase off an alligator and feed its chick on the lake shore.

There are links to many of the devices discussed below in the **Inventory** chapter for those who want to purchase them. Decide what you need, buy it before you leave, test it, and use it until you are very familiar with it. Many times a cell phones, cameras, watches or radios have saved someone's life. A boy in Florida snapped a picture of the man that was trying to pull him into a truck to kidnap him. The villain let go of the boy and drove away quickly in a panic. A firefighter in Yellowstone, separated from his training team, used a small transistor radio to distract a crazed bear long enough to climb a tree to safety. A young lady hiker lost in Death Valley got online using her Internet enabled phone and reached the park headquarters to ask for help. Without it she would have surely died of thirst.

If you take the time to be familiar with your equipment it will more than pay for itself. Good equipment will enable you to go further, go safely, and go for less money. The catch is; you have to have the technology with you. You must know how to use it. It must be powered up and in good working condition for it to benefit you.

While in the wilderness if you are hiking and tent camping a day's walk from your van, consider the use of two way radios for communication with each other. They are cheap to buy and the batteries can last for weeks. There are no airtime charges and usually nothing hinders the reception. The technology behind these radios does not change from year to year so you won't have to buy new ones like you do cell phones and computers. They work without cell phone tower access.

GPS enabled devices like a Garmin, an Internet enabled cell phone, a specialty watch, or a portable computer enable you to know exactly where you are whether walking or driving. Take note of the coordinates of where you want to go *and* where you parked your van so you can get to both places. It does you no good to know where you are if you don't know where that is *in relation to where you want to be*. Carefully manage your power consumption with each of these devices. Dead batteries equal disaster.

When using your cell phone as your primary communication and navigational device make sure and test the connection every two hours. If you spend the night in a submerged canyon deep in the mountains and need to call for help during an emergency, only to realize at that critical moment in the dark that you do not have a connection, someone could die.

Some use a Citizens Band Radio commonly called a CB radio installed in the van to communicate with hundreds of thousands of professional truckers and drivers making deliveries all over the country. The range can be as much as 30 miles. The help they give is invaluable and often instantaneous. Simply pick up the radio microphone and say for example "4 wheeler heading south on highway 123 looking for the best barbeque restaurant in the next 30 miles, drivers can you help please?" Professional truckers call themselves *"drivers"* and they call anyone in a personal vehicle a *"four wheeler".* If you use their lingo you will get help immediately nearly every time. My wife and I drove a tractor-trailer together and would talk for hours with other drivers about many different subjects. CB radios provide great, cheap fun, and valuable free information. Do not install a big tall whip style antennae permanently on your Vanabode unless you do not plan on doing any city based stealth camping. It draws too much attention to the vehicle.

We use a wireless card in our laptop computer to stay connected to the Internet even when staying for a month at a time in rugged national parks like Glacier and Zion. There is a certain awesome reality to hiking with your travel mate all day into the interior of some completely wild and untamed forest, and then getting online to check your email, pay bills, and read the day's news when you get back to your van that night. All major networks have this capability now so for a few bucks a month you can be online anywhere you have a cell phone connection. This is how I personally make money while traveling (http://www.marketingmakesmoney.com). You can get this same connectivity straight through your cell phone and then tether a laptop to it using an external cable. This is an example of letting technology free you, rather than tie you down.

High tech gadgets do have limitations though so never be without a simple paper map of the area you are hiking, the city you are exploring, or the state you are in. If you pay a small annual fee to become a member of AAA, you will get discounts nearly everywhere, as well as unlimited free maps that you can pick up from any AAA office in the country. My wife and I have fun pouring over a large full color map of a hundred mile area, discussing where we want to go, where to park, where we want to swim, how far we can drive versus how far we can hike, the terrain, the weather, and the geography of lakes, rivers, hills, forests, prairies, deserts and mountains. I have information on many other highly specialized and cheap travel books and guides online (http://www.vanabode.com/camp/amazon-travel-store.htm). Some of these show thousands of free places to camp. Some show thousands of places to get a shower, or park for free, or get in the water.

You can download the FREE goggle earth app for your computer or cellular phone and see all the typography in America. Use this with a local topographic map and you will not have any problems finding great places to camp off the grid for free.

Discretion

Discretion is very important when Vanaboding. Since many people have purchased my book some cities like San Francisco have implemented laws trying to restrict people from *sleeping in their vehicles.* Why? Because city governments make money from taxing people, homeowners, and businesses. Vanaboding removes this major expense from your life and they don't like it one bit. They want your money. This is at odds with my goal, empowering you to get your life back. The first step: stop giving your money away to every entity with its hand out. With a Vanabode you can avoid the financial rape and pillage and rampant over taxation of today.

There are three main issues to address when it comes to discretion. Some people call it stealth camping. It is one of the most important elements of traveling on $20 a day unless you stay only in the wilderness. 1) Do not look like you are sleeping in your van. 2) Do not talk about sleeping in your van. 3) Choose locations where you will be left alone. As Ed Buryn, an American vagabonding pioneer said, "Be free, but act normal around the others."

For clandestine travel I recommend a van exactly like the one shown and described in the **Van** chapter. Notice the van is plain white, non-attention grabbing, with no external indications that someone is using it for sleeping, housing or camping. There are no roof racks, awnings, air conditioners, stove or hot water heater vents, bicycle racks, or RV windows. It looks like thousands of other work vans used all over the country. We have windows only in the back doors. This buys us privacy, security, and most importantly, less attention. It looks like a work van not a camping van.

When parked in the city we put up the windshield cover, keep windows and doors shut and locked, and use the curtains inside. These curtains cannot be easily seen because they are behind dark tinted glass. Reference the **Van** chapter for more on this.

Retail stores like Wal-Mart, Sam's Club and the Great Outdoors let people "rest" in the parking lot overnight but so many RVers abuse this privilege it is hard to tell how long it will last. In my travel bookstore (http://www.vanabode.com/camp/amazon-travel-store.htm) you will find books that locate hundreds of thousands of places you can park legally overnight hassle free. The key is to be discrete. Do not give anyone a reason to approach your vehicle. Do not draw attention. Move the van to a different parking spot each morning if staying for more than a day in one place.

We were in south Florida for three months one winter so we rotated around from mall parking lots, to Wal-Mart and Sam's club parking lots, to public parks, to library parking lots, as well as 24 hour restaurants, hotels and book store areas. We did this so as not to draw undue attention from management or the police. It worked well. Instead of paying $210 per night for a hotel room or $6,000 for the 3 month busy tourist season for a condo rental we stayed for $17 a day TOTAL including food, gas and lodging. Or cost was lower than normal because we spent our days at the beach and did not drive long distances much.

Remember people don't want hassles. So don't hassle them. You are living a fun alternative lifestyle free of nearly all expenses. Don't rub other people's noses in it. *Don't force the police or other authorities to notice you.* Vanabode quietly. As stated in the **Sleep** chapter, *only twice in 20+ years* of Vanaboding have the police ever politely knocked on the van door and asked what we were doing.

It may sound crazy but I once saw some retirees set up a giant motorhome in the parking lot of a Sam's Club in Florida. They opened the doors, put out the steps, opened up the 10 foot awning, put down the leveling jacks, and actually had a couple of lawn chairs outside the camper *in the parking lot in full view of all the shoppers and store management*. I actually watched them take their scruffy mongrel dog over to the grassy area between two sections of the lot and let it defecate on the turf. They were not allowed to stay long. They were told to leave. I know, because we were allowed to stay. We watched management personally ask them to leave. We quietly and discretely stayed there for a full month, hassle free, when visiting my children in Florida and wanting to be near the beach for daily access.

If you talk about what you are doing, others become jealous or discover that they cannot make any money from you, and become hostile. In the **Hygiene** chapter for example, I explained that when you are staying somewhere for a month or longer you should purchase a health or fitness club membership. Then you can shower and use the bathroom, gym, and swimming pools every day. However if you plan on being there less than a week you *do not want them to know* that you will *not* be buying the annual membership. Don't talk too much.

Talking up the lifestyle can lead to misunderstandings from friends if you don't handle it correctly. We often stay with friends when traveling. We have had a lot of fun doing this. We pitch in and buy groceries and take our hosts out to dinner or lunch while we are there. Our hosts, be it family or acquaintances, seem to love the time together as much as we do. We often stay for as long as a week, exploring the area, based out of our host friend's house.

Most of the time though our hosts are working all day and are often committed to mortgages, kids, clubs, businesses, and debts that prevent them from traveling as they would like. So, while we are staying with them we do not rub it in. We do not sit around and talk about how *great we have it*. We too had debts and mortgages at one time so we know how it feels. We worked hard for a few years to get out of debt but not everyone is in the same place at the same time. Someday we too may not be able to roam about.

So be sensitive. Be discrete. Do not constantly talk about Vanaboding and how much fun you are having doing it. Don't be selfish. Don't be a know it all. Instead show some interest in them by asking about their lives. Do not overstay your welcome.

Destination choices are important. Finding the right places that offer your style of fun is a big part of experiencing the kind of adventure and romance that Vanaboding affords. We have hundreds of destination reports in the private online Vanabode Destinations pages. (http://www.vanabode.com/travel/destinations.htm) These pages detail our experiences while we were there, including the good and bad, temperatures, time of year to visit, pictures, videos, parking advice, and budget information.

Always appear to be on a casual camping trip, not living in your van full time. Or you can refer to the BOOK section of camping resources (http://www.vanabode.com/camp/amazon-travel-store.htm) on the Internet for information on hundreds of thousands of acres of BLM land where you can camp forever for free and not have to worry about stealth camping. I also list resources that cover strategies for hanging out at casinos in nearly every state, lifetime memberships that allow for staying two weeks a year free at thousands of full amenity campgrounds, enjoying big world class festivals like *Burning Man* or Sturgis, and using specialty campgrounds for $10 night.

Budget

The less money you spend, the less time you are tied to a job working in one boring location. Now, since you're working less, you suddenly have more time to play. The less money you make the less taxes you pay. Some people spend their entire early years in school getting some degree so they can work in one place paying off the school loans and a mortgage for the rest of their life. Why? So they can buy stuff! HUH? Buy stuff? That's it? That's what they are spending their entire life's worth of time on?

Current American culture teaches you should get more money, to buy more things, by spending more of your precious time, getting more education, so you can get a better job, and work until you are old, and have saved enough money, to buy it all. May I suggest that the years you give up *doing all that* are not worth the price of your irreplaceable youth? You are not improved if you are smarter or richer than you were last year, if you forget that you are also deader.

You are making a huge mistake if you are spending your most precious irreplaceable gift: your time; working to buy garages full of junk, houses full of knickknacks and stupid Earth polluting machines like lawnmowers, second and third cars, off road vehicles, boats, weed whackers, edgers, mixers, can openers, vacuum cleaners, washing machines, dryers, hair dryers, curling irons, cd players, televisions, blenders, juicers, grills, smokers, electric slicers, heaters, air conditioners, hot water heaters, microwaves, stoves, ovens, toasters, cell phones, computers, etc.

You should realize the things you really want are much simpler than what the sellers of all this junk lead you to believe. Example: You don't want a noisy, expensive, complicated, washing machine that is eventually going to wear out. You want clean clothes. You don't really want to sit in front of the television brain dead the last 2 hours of your day. You do that because you are working so hard to *pay* for the television, cable, Internet, and the house to put it in, that you don't have the energy left for anything else. The end result is you get fatter, sadder, bored and run down.

This Mexican Fisherman's story makes the same point I am making. A fishing boat was docked in a tiny coastal village south of the border. An American tourist complimented the local fisherman on the quality of his fish and asked how long it took to catch them. "Not long", said the fisherman. "Then why didn't you stay out longer and catch more?" asked the American. The man said that his small catch was enough for his family. The American asked, "What do you do with the rest of your time?" The fisherman replied, *"I sleep late, play with my children, catch a few fish, and take a siesta with my wife. In the evenings I go into the village to see my friends, have a few drinks, play the guitar and sing a few songs. I have fun."* The American interrupted, "Stop. I have a Master's degree from Duke. I can help you. Start by fishing longer. Sell the extra fish you catch to buy a bigger boat. The larger boat will bring in more money so you can buy a second one and a third one and so on until you have an entire fleet. Skip the middleman and sell directly to the processing plants. Then you can leave this little village, move to Mexico City or New York City and from there you can direct your enterprise." "How long would that take?" asked the fisherman? "20-25 years", replied the American. "And after that?" asked the fisherman. "That's when it gets even better", answered the smiling American. "When your business gets really big, start selling stocks and make millions!" "Millions? Really? And after that?" asked the fisherman. . . *"After that you'll be able to retire, live in a tiny coastal village, sleep late, play with your grandchildren, catch a few fish, take a siesta with your wife and spend your evenings drinking and playing the guitar with friends!"* It's full circle. Some of you totally get it. For those still confused I offer my theme song. *Prioritize Your Pleasure.* Skip all the garbage most people spend the first 40 years of their lives struggling for, and jump right to what you are really after. Live now. The key to this sustainable travel budget I propose is the elimination of hundreds of expenses from your life. This enables you to prioritize your pleasure on a small budget.

You never have to pay for airfare, hotel rooms, rental cars, travel or tour guides, mortgage payments, utility bills, real estate taxes, homeowners insurance, water bills, sewage bills, home owners association dues, house repairs, furniture, cable bills, internet connection, pest control, yard maintenance, appliance repairs, fancy wardrobes, etc. Managing your bankroll and travel budget is essential if you want to travel a long time without work, travel far on limited savings, or travel forever.

Being frugal can be fun. Every *single* dollar you do not spend is about *two* dollars you don't have to earn (taxes, work related costs like wardrobe, car, etc. usually leave you with about one dollar for every two that you earn from the job).

You can live happy and completely satisfied while spending very little. Here's how. First, pick a budget range. For example my wife and I have traveled on budgets where we spent an average of $12 a day total for the both of us. We have also traveled expensively where we averaged $90 a day. We have found our sweet spot and are happiest at a $40 a day budget ($20 each). We only exceed that if we are hitting some elaborate venue like a museum that charges $20 a head admission or if we are driving a very long distance in a short time: something I discourage.

Our *daily average* typically breaks down like this - $11 in gas to drive about 70 miles; $5 in park entrance fees, parking, tolls, bus fare, oil changes; $13 for one good shared restaurant meal usually lunch; $7 for food purchased from grocery stores, farmers markets, and roadside stands; $2 budgeted daily for cell phone usage; $2 saved daily for van expenses like license renewal and vehicle insurance.

This budget is just a range. Sometimes we sit in one spot for a week, so we obviously would not be spending $11 a day on gasoline. If there are no interesting restaurants nearby, we spend all the food money at the farmers market on super nutritious organic foods rather than spending the majority of our budget on a big dinner out. We often stay in or just outside of national parks for a month or longer. $400 covers campsites and showers and $300 is spent on food. This comes to an average of just $12 a day for each of us. Try that at home.

Our overhead is so low compared to a typical American's 9 to 5 grind lifestyle that we are able to really enjoy our money and what we buy with it. Some people spend as little as $10 a day; others have the income or savings to blow $125 a day or more. Decide for yourself how much you want to spend and on what you want to spend it. But remember never budget less than what you need for the 5 *Essentials of a Great Life.*

Multiply what you spend daily by the number of days you want to be out to see the amount you need in the bank when you first take off. If you plan on spending $50 a day and be out for 20 days then you need $1,000. Obviously if you have a steady income that covers your daily Vanabode expenses then you won't have to worry about money at all. In the **Making Money While Traveling** chapter I list resources that lead to hundreds of ways to make money while on the road or at home including how I have been doing it since 2004.

Here is a list of other money saving strategies for those on a limited budget.

After you finish your meal, ask the fast food restaurant cashier if you can have an extra packet of ketchup, salt, sugar, pepper, sprinkle on cheese, mustard, paper towel, napkin, plastic fork, spoon, knife, jelly, or honey. These take up less room in your cooler. Storing large containers of condiments like mustard and ketchup is not a wise use of space. Stay in a big hotel and ask the maid if you can have an extra set of shampoo, conditioner, soap, toilet paper and lotion when leaving.

I highly recommend you investigate the FREE wireless phone (http://www.vanabode.com/camp/free-government-supported-phone.htm) and FREE monthly plan including text and talk minutes. At one point I had this phone and plan and it was absolutely wonderful. The battery would last for two weeks without a single charge. The plan included plenty of free minutes. The exceptional service was by Tracfone, the biggest in the business, providing perfect reception in the most far out places. This is not a smart phone however, so it cannot replace a GPS or web enabled phone for mapping out a trip or as a logistical device.

Buy the annual National Park pass (costs about 40 cents a day) and it will get you into ALL national parks for one year for free. Then you can usually get water, maps, showers, toilet usage and fantastic adventures for nearly nothing.

Do not drive further than you need to. The further you drive the more tired you get and the more money you spend on fuel. Everyone always thinks that the great adventurous and cool places are always thousands of miles away. That is not true. For example we have friends in Florida that spend their only 7 days off every year flying to some crowded tourist filled beach in a foreign land "because the Bahamas or Puerto Rico or Mexico is so beautiful". I don't know of one of them that has ever driven the 35 miles to explore one of the greatest super pristine private beaches in the world, Playalinda (http://www.rvforsaleguide.com/playalinda-clothing-optional-beach-florida.htm) You can swim with massive green sea turtles, manatees, and manta rays in water visibility to 30 feet, catch fresh fish right from the beach and sunbathe nude privately all day. I wrote about this secret Florida beach years ago. I could live there for 60 days on the same $2,000 others spend for 7 days of vacation.

Buy locally grown foods from vendors and farmers markets. It is cheaper, healthier, more fun, and easier to do than scheduling a big restaurant sitting. These small mom and pop stands don't have big overhead or shipping costs so the food costs less even though it is fresher. We often barter for bruised or *less than perfect* items and get them even cheaper.

Some people take a white towel so they look like a hotel guest and discretely jump in a hotel swimming pool, and then shower off and leave. In Vegas this is perfectly legal, and encouraged at many casino pools (they hope while you are there enjoying the day that you may be coaxed into buying a drink, food, or renting a cabana.) Some places may hassle you if you do this. Baths can be free.

Some people eat for free in places like pubs, bars, clubs, conventions, and hotel lobbies. They usually give away free appetizers and finger food during happy hour. They simply wander in grab some, buy a drink if they really want one, or just eat and leave. All the locals are doing it. That is what the food is there for, to bring in prospective customers. They are a prospective customer. You can also eat at the big chain stores like Sam's Club and Whole Foods where they usually have 7-10 sample trays open throughout the store.

Cooking with the solar oven I recommend in the **Inventory** and **Food** chapters is free. If you are camp fire cooking get free firewood from dumpsters or trash dumps. Things like furniture, old crates, books, etc., burn quite easily. You can also get wood from abandoned campsites, and in the surrounding forest. You can take old newspapers, roll them up *very tight*, soak in water, put bungee cords around them to keep them tight, and then dry your new *logs* in the sun. You can easily cook a quick meal with these.

Restaurants are where my wife and I tend to splurge. We spend the biggest portion of our budget eating great meals everywhere we go. But you don't have to. Nearly every city, especially the smaller ones, has some kind of lunch buffet usually priced at $5 to $8 each. Some people pig out for an hour and are satisfied all day on the one meal. Some food places have mini bars for free. For example nearly all the Mexican joints out West have condiment bars where you can have as much as you want of good stuff like: Pico de Gallo, pickled vegetables, exotic salsas, sliced tomatoes and peppers, marinated onions and carrots, and more. Buy a $2 taco, get a free water, and then enjoy the side stuff for free. It is cheap, healthy, and delicious.

Free entertainment can be found everywhere. See this special Las Vegas site for example (http://www.alasvegasdeal.com/lasvegas-nightclubs.htm). Simply wander around between 9 pm and 11:30 pm in front of one of the top nightclubs with the girl in your group dressed nice. A club *spotter* will approach you with free early bird passes. These clubs typically charge up to $90 per person to get in, but during the first two hours of opening they just want to fill it up with people they hope will buy booze. These are the most incredible clubs in the world. You get in for free, dance until you cannot move, sponge bathe off in the bathroom real quick, then Vanabode sleep in the parking lot until the next morning. Consult the Las Vegas part of the Vanabode Destinations (http://www.vanabode.com/travel/destinations.htm) section for total coverage of how to get much more for free in the greatest city in the world, including free rooms, free pool passes, exciting tours, complimentary buffets, great food and discounted show tickets.

Another one of our favorite things to do when visiting new cities is to investigate what almost all cultural centers call "locals appreciation day". Those that run the museums, art galleries, botanical gardens, cultural centers, specialty parks, and natural history museums, all realize that many locals cannot afford the entrance fee. So usually one day a month is designated as "free admission day". Call each place you find in the local phone book, online, or in the local tourist guide, and ask which day is free. These places are nearly always so awesome that they represent one of the single greatest bargains you will ever experience while traveling. Make good plans. Take the time to see the big sights in each town for free.

Information is imperative. Check with the chamber of commerce, tourist information centers, and welcome centers when *first setting out* to explore a new city or place. This will save time and money and eliminate frustration. Do not waste time wandering around. You will be bored and end up crossing some cool place off your list and saying "saw that" when you really didn't see anything at all. Did you ask a local where to find the absolute best meal under $10? Did you walk all the bigger parks, or hike the prettiest areas, or shop in the retail stores unique to that area, or enjoy the outdoors, be it in the water or in the forest? Did you find out where cheap happy hours are with free finger food? Did you ask about free live music or art galleries or public tours? Did you get directions to these places and experience them?

They can be super fun and very cheap but you won't know about them unless you ask.

Only the more expensive venues can afford to advertise in newspapers and local magazines.

This is how we enjoy things even locals in an area never see. Why? Because the locals don't have the *time* to enjoy these things even though they live right there. Why? Because they are working so many hours that when they get off work, all they want to do is go home and rest. We on the other hand are time rich! This is the single greatest message I can give you.

Being time rich is a thousand times more important than being money rich. The rich say they can buy whatever they want. They lie. They can't. Most of them are so busy investing, and protecting their money, and maintaining all the stuff they have purchased, and avoiding scams and people trying to sue them or steal from them, that they have little time for anything else. Most never understand that the very best thing they can do with their money is *buy their life back!*

Don't buy a bigger house or another car or boat or some other pathetic toy. Take the $20,000 you have saved and Vanabode for 18 months. It will be the absolute highlight of your entire life. You will never forget it. This is real budgeting. Determine what it is you enjoy doing and do it! If loved ones don't want to go; convince them. If they can't afford to go; pay their way. If they are scared to go; make them read this book. If they still will not cooperate; consider going without them. Make memories that will last forever. Take pictures. Journal about it. I will even pay you for your travel reports if you like. See the money making page (http://www.vanabode.com/camp/quit-your-job-make-money.htm) on the Internet for more info. This is your life: is it what you want it to be?

"The one satisfied with the least feels the richest." *Jason Odom*

Mail and State Residency

If you are only traveling for a short period of time ask your neighbors, friends or family to forward your mail to you whenever you need it. If you are staying somewhere long, acquire the local address for the post office in the town you are in, and have your friends forward your mail to that post office care of *general delivery* and your name. The post office will typically need about 3-4 days to receive *general delivery.* If you do *not* want to hang around 3-4 days waiting for it plan ahead. Call the post office *where you plan to be in 3-4 days* and give *that* address to your friends so they can forward your mail *ahead of time.* Then your mail will be waiting for you when you get there, and you can leave that town when you wish, rather than waiting for mail to arrive. Not all Post Offices' accept general delivery mail but most do. Post offices will not hold your general delivery mail for a long time so be prompt in picking it up.

Since we are often gone to certain areas for 3-6 months at a time, I hired a full-time mail service to handle all my mail. It is best to use a Mail Service company near your residence if you are going to keep one up. They receive all of our mail including important items like personal tax returns, insurance documents, automobile license tag renewal, and more. This company operates year round for us, they receive our mail, and forward or overnight it via FedEx or UPS to whatever address we give them wherever we are.

Sometimes we have them forward our mail to a local post office via General Delivery, to a friend's house, or to the physical address of a campground in the area where we are staying at the time. Then we just ask the front desk at the campground for our mail and show our ID to claim it. We always have a tracking number as a backup against loss since the company puts all our mail in one common envelope or box.

This is a cheap, easy, safe way to get your mail. It keeps mail from backing up wherever you normally receive mail (which can invite theft). Plus you don't have to bother your family or friends or give up any of your mail privacy.

The most important mail often consists of bills coming due. Avoid that and pay everything online. Set up automatic deduction to pay bills from a credit card. The credit card companies protect you against theft. You can also manually or automatically pay nearly any bill at each individual merchant's website from your checking account if you set it up beforehand. Simply bring along your personal computer or Internet enabled cell phone to get access once a month.

By doing this I have eliminated nearly every conceivable mail related hassle cheaply and easily. Now I can travel unfettered and with a clear mind knowing all my affairs are in order. I know I am not missing out on any important mail.

If you give up all stationary base camp dwellings like a house entirely, you will need to decide what state you will call *home;* even though you may spend little time there annually. This is called state residency. Choose a mail service company in the state you choose to be a resident of. You will often need that "mailing address" that you're paying for when you fill out the actual state residency form, proving that you *live* there.

Some states are cheaper to base out of than others. Some states require you to have your vehicle inspected every year. This costs you money and becomes a huge inconvenience. Some don't have state income taxes, which will save you lots of money you can use for traveling. Some offer Medicare to low-income families that you may qualify for in one state but not the other. Some have super cheap annual vehicle registration fees while others can be over $900 a year just to *renew* your tag.

Some states or cities have substantially cheaper automotive insurance than others saving you thousands of dollars a year. I once moved from Las Vegas in Clark County Nevada to Pahrump Nevada in Nye County just 45 minutes away. My automobile insurance dropped instantly from $1,600 a year to $590 a year without changing insurance companies. I have found Nevada, Florida, South Dakota, and Delaware (because it is cheap to incorporate a business here as well), to be the best choices. You will need to investigate the states that make sense for you so that you end up with the best solution. If you get it wrong the first time don't worry, you can always change it later.

Laundry

Laundry chores depend on personal daily activities and choices concerning climate and temperature. Most people would like to eliminate laundry altogether. Vanaboding is perfect for this since the clothes needed to do most activities can be reused over and over throughout the week without any problems.

Despite what you see on television, life is not a fashion show. People aren't walking around concerned about what you are wearing. For everything except big city trips encompassing museums, concerts, clubs, fancy restaurants, parties, and the like, you will probably use and reuse 2-5 sets of outdoor clothes that fit your desired comfort level. I have been on many 30-60 day trips where I wore one pair of good quality sandals over 90% of the time. That eliminates socks. It is much cooler to wear shorts without undergarments. That eliminates underwear. Many trips I rotate through 5 pairs of nylon shorts for a week or two. This means I don't have to wash heavy difficult to dry jeans. Eliminate unnecessary items to reduce laundry work.

The breathable sports shirts sold nearly everywhere are perfect for hiking. The long sleeved ones eliminate the need for the application of bug spray and sunscreens while keeping you shaded and cool as they wick away sweat. Later you can easily rinse these lightweight fabrics out along with your synthetic nylon shorts and wring them out to dry in the van. This eliminates trips to the Laundromat.

Many weeks our days are spent on long hikes wearing synthetic shorts or long loose nylon like pants for keeping bugs and thorns away. Obviously we will go through a pair of socks on these days. When we get back to the van we stuff the dirty clothes into one of the plastic storage containers under the bed. When we run out of clothes we simply visit a Laundromat for an hour and wash and dry everything.

Sometimes we go for nearly a month without hitting a Laundromat by simply rinsing out our clothes after each use. We use sinks, a tub in our van, streams, lakes, oceans, rivers, water hoses at gas stations, and anywhere else there is water. Then we hang the clothes to dry on a bungee cord either inside or outside the van. Sometimes if air flow is good I lay clothes on the dash where the sun will dry them quickly.

I have also used the vertically located dash vents to dry my clothes while driving, by running the air conditioner and laying the damp clothes over the vents. Do NOT lay clothes over the vents that face *up* as the condensation could run down into the duct system and cause problems. When we are at friends' houses, at a hotel room, renting a truck stop shower, or showering at a campground, we take a few clothing items into the shower with us and *do laundry* while we bathe. Simply place the wet clothes in a plastic bag when exiting and hang up to dry.

Another effective strategy is to take a small airtight container like a Tupperware bowl with a tight fitting lid. Put your dirty clothing item in the bowl, fill 80% with water, drip in one drop of liquid soap, and seal the lid. Then shake the bowl for 2 minutes or simply drive for about an hour and the clothes will wash themselves. Complete this process twice for the same item using a change of water to get it extra clean.

There are many ways to wash clothes and get them clean. It is more important though to choose the proper kind of clothing to begin with. Don't gravitate to what you are used to wearing. Purchase what works best for your new life. Buy what works for the geographic conditions of the area you will be spending the most time in. Think about the activities you will be doing as well when choosing your wardrobe.

National Park Camping Issues

The National Parks and State run recreational areas in the United States are extraordinary. They are unequaled in terms of ease of use, price, geographic diversity, and overall experience. However, they require special strategies when exploring. If you want to get the most out of them you can't just show up and hope for the best. You will be disappointed for sure. I hear idiots all the time say something like "I've been to Yellowstone already, been there, done that". Really? I don't think so. I usually find out they literally spent *one day* driving around a few miles of the millions of acres of Yellowstone wilderness back when they were 16 years old. They tried to take in this national treasure from the back seat of their parent's car in 8 hours of daylight. Pathetic.

If you plan carefully, and follow the suggestions below, you can actually have real experiences that lead to real memories that you will never, ever forget. You can have an extraordinary time in a place set aside because of its incredible diversity, beauty, and rugged uniqueness.

My suggestions are explained in greater detail below; but here's the short version. Do not fail to visit camping spots adjacent to, but not within, the big parks boundaries. Always buy the annual pass if you are visiting more than one park a year. Visit during the off-season. Always plan at least ten days in any one park. Make reservations for camping spots well ahead of time. Stock up early. Play by the rules.

Proximity camping has been good for us. Most big national parks are surrounded by other national forests, state forests, and scenic areas, which have basically the same climate, wilderness, and interesting terrain as the big more popular park. We often go camping in these areas and experience nearly the same things as we would have enjoyed within the bigger more well-known national park boundaries. These *adjacent* wilderness areas have some advantages though. They cost less. They are always less crowded. They are less regulated. They are quieter and more private. They are often just as much fun.

To proximity camp, simply spend the night just *outside* the big national park. Then drive into the national park the next morning to go on any special hikes that lead to popular possibly more spectacular things like a famous waterfall or herd of buffalo. Then drive back out and camp for free on the outskirts of the national park in the evenings.

Buy the annual park pass at the first national park you visit. It gives you free *admission* for an entire year to all the National Parks in the United States and some recreation areas. It is a real money saver if you plan on park hopping or Vanaboding through all of them during a years' time. You must present the actual plastic card *and* a form of personal official picture identification that *matchs* it when passing through the park entrances. You cannot borrow someone else's to get in. This annual admission pass does NOT include discounted or free camping. It only provides for admission onto the property. While Vanaboding an annual pass combined with proximity camping provides the best balance of convenience, budget, and fun.

Visit during the off-season or you will often be disappointed. When parks are crowded they are noisy. They feel polluted from all the car traffic and extra campfires burning. During the busy season they are more expensive, and the wildlife often hides because of the increased human activity. It is easier to get reservations during the off-season. You will often have better weather too. The off-season is more fun as well unless you want thousands of people around you.

Make reservations. Many parks are so controlled that not one single vehicle can be parked anywhere without a permit sticker on the dash. We were in Yellowstone one time and I had a small 23-foot class C recreational vehicle. I did not want to pay for a campsite and be crowded up with a hundred other noisy people. So I thought I would just wait until it got dark and pull off into the wilderness somewhere. WRONG. Those rangers were all over me. They chased us from one spot to another, every time, the same thing "sir you cannot stay here overnight, exit the park or go to your reserved camping spot".

Finally after driving around and getting chased all over for two hours I gave up and went to the gigantic Yellowstone Lodge. We ate an overpriced dinner there. I figured I would stay in the parking lot overnight. WRONG. Signs were posted all over that said, "No overnight parking", vehicles will be towed. Sure enough, as the hour got later and later all the cars disappeared out of the parking lot except for three employees' cars and my RV.

It was 11 pm. I was tired. It was at least a 2 hour drive from the exit gates of the park so I made a sign that said "RV won't start, will have it towed in the morning, staying with friends in the Lodge" and hung it on the windshield. I lifted up the hood of the RV and left a cable hanging out of the engine area. Within an hour a ranger and officer came by and banged on the door and told us we had to move the RV.

We just pretended that we were not inside and they eventually left. I assume they believed the sign I made about my RV being disabled. I got away with it, but it took hours to pull off. They could have still given me a costly ticket. I spent extra fuel driving around. I was frustrated. I won't do it again. If I had planned for *where I was going to spend the night* earlier, I would not have had these national park specific problems.

Stock up. Purchase all food and supplies well before you get within 100 miles of the park. All stores, shops, information centers, welcome centers, etc. will get increasingly more expensive the closer you get to the entrance. I have seen gasoline and milk for sale at more than $7 per gallon and flimsy windbreaker jackets costing over $50 at the convenience stores under contract *within* park boundaries. I hardly call that convenience. I have seen parks hand out $40 fines for picking up firewood from the ground while simultaneously selling firewood at the canteen store for $9 per bundle. The unprepared completely waste their money. They often end up paying amounts that are nearly inconceivable.

Play by the rules within any large government managed national park. Weekend warriors staff the parks during the busy season. They are very passionate about keeping the tourists in line. Many hand out real fines that must be paid within 30 days of leaving the park. There are many ways for them to get your money. If you allow wildlife to get into your food, litter, park in an area where it is not allowed, make excessive noise, or make a fire when it is prohibited, they will fine you and steal your fun faster than you can say Smokey Bear.

Skip the expensive national parks altogether if you want to. Some live for free in places like Slab City for months. Slab City was originally a Marine Corp training camp called Camp Dunlap. It is located south of Joshua Tree national park off Interstate 10. After they closed the base, hundreds of people moved in to stabilize and colonize the concrete slabs left behind. This is wild unforgiving desert for most of the year, but in the cooler months it can be fun mainly because it is free.

Slab City hosts many seriously offbeat characters. Some people here use massive nets over their motorhomes to minimize the blazing sun and wind. Others setup Internet café's where you can connect to the World Wide Web using their connections for a few bucks. Others have actually planted vegetables and bring in water in giant tanks to support small gardens. Bring lots of water, as there are no sources of public water on site unless someone happens to be there selling it.

Weather

If the snake bites *before* it is charmed, there is no profit for the charmer. Timing the weather and temperature are *extremely* important to happy Vanabode travels. Plan and practice good timing to experience the kind of weather, temperature, climate, and precipitation that help make any length journey fun and hassle free.

Weather problems are quite easy to handle. Stay informed via radio, television or the Internet. If fires are raging in southern California, or the highways are closed in the Northeast due to ice and snow, or a drought in Georgia is drying up all the lakes, or a hurricane is brewing in Florida, then common sense dictates you steer clear. The great thing about Vanaboding is you *can* go elsewhere. When danger is imminent simply drive away.

I have often done this and it has worked perfectly with zero loss to my lifestyle and belongings. I left Florida numerous times 3-5 days before the hurricanes of the past 14 years made landfall, while every other person was scrambling to board up, and spending a lot of money doing it. When they were done they were stuck with all the damage, inconvenience, and costs that the insurance companies didn't cover. Later they all paid increased insurance premiums for filing a claim. Meantime we are off having fun because we timed our adventure to avoid the disaster. We return when we feel like it; when the cities have their infrastructure back together.

One time before Vanabode, during one of Florida's most devastating hurricanes, my wife and I parked our Class A motorhome behind a grocery store on the side of the building protected from the wind. I remember my brother coming up there hours before the storm hit to tell us we were crazy and to come stay with him in his big house. Bad timing for that though.

That same year we had already sat through two other hurricanes, one in my mother's house and one in my wife's mother's house. Being closed up in a hot, muggy, humid, house without air-conditioning, sleeping on makeshift beds, sharing bathrooms with toilets that don't flush for 4 days straight, and rationing water was not our idea of fun. I declined my brother's generous offer and instead pulled the RV tight up against the buildings 20-foot tall back wall. The hurricane smashed into the city. We barely felt the wind at all. It was quite fun watching people's yard art and furniture fly by horizontal to us at 90 miles per hour. We'd cry out "Hey was that a shopping cart?" "No, I think it was a kids swing set", "No, it couldn't be, looked more like a bicycle!"

Every one we knew that was living in typical houses lost electricity. Most lived a hot miserable existence for 8 days straight. Our life went on uninterrupted though because we were mobile. We had options. For some reason the commercial store where we were parked did not lose electricity, though they did remain closed for a week. So, we plugged our RV into the grocery store's outdoor electrical outlet and had air conditioning, television, computer access, hot meals, a cold refrigerator, good sleep and awesome views of the devastation happening 100 feet away. The police drove by every 8 hours or so to check on us and just smiled though the rainy windows of their cruisers.

Many years ago I told everyone at my job that I did not have a house but lived in my motorhome. They just stared. Then one of the guys who had just got his first 30-year mortgage on a worn out 40-year-old house in Satellite Beach exclaimed "why would anyone pay $250,000 for *that* when they could buy a house?" He was referencing the rich retirees he knew that were buying $250,000 diesel Class A motorhomes.

I explained they did it because they *could*, because a motorhome is *vastly superior to a house* in many ways, because living mobile is *super fun*. He just stared at me in disbelief. Now though, his house is worth 40% less than what he owes on it, his insurance, maintenance, taxes, mortgage payments, HOA fees and repairs keep him jailed to his job: probably for another 20 years. He never questions me now.

Temperature is something that is of paramount importance to us. This is one of the few issues that demand careful planning if you want to Vanabode happily. I cannot sleep, make love, eat, rest, or even read a book if it is much over 80 degrees. When I speak of the awesome times in Las Vegas, Arizona, California, New Mexico and Florida in the Destinations Guide (http://www.vanabode.com/travel/destinations.htm) I do so with timing in mind. You *cannot* go to these places during the wrong time of year unless you are paying for a camping site with electrical hookup for air conditioning.

For example, you cannot enjoy Vanaboding in Florida in the summer. It is impossibly hot and muggy. Your bed sheets stay damp all day, the bugs eat you alive, and there is nowhere to hide. The pools, oceans, lakes and rivers can only give temporary respite. They are beautiful and fun to play in, but when it comes to sleeping or resting comfortably, they are worthless.

My wife is somewhat colder blooded than I. She needs it warm enough at night that she is not sleeping stiff and curled up in defense against the cold. One time we traveled through Albuquerque, New Mexico at night visiting some of her family and we overnighted in the Walmart parking lot. We nearly froze to death with only a sheet and small bedspread over us. My wife had tights and numerous shirts on but when it hit 26 degrees that night not even our rabbit Bugsy was moving. He just curled up in a ball and would not budge even when we picked him up.

At 4 am we had finally had enough. Neither of us had any rest. We were more tired than when we went to bed 8 hours prior. We lay there all night like dummy mummies, shivering and hoping we would eventually get warm. We never did. We learned our lesson. We got up and bought a 10-degree sleeping bag from the store for $29. The next night we put that over us, warmed up in 15 minutes, and slept soundly all night. Problem solved. Some people love sleeping with a winter cap or hooded sweatshirt. Keep your head and feet warm and you will not be cold elsewhere. Temperature is one of the most important elements of good sleep.

So, do not travel anywhere and expect to live happily, if it is too cold, too wet, too muggy, too rainy, too hot, or too windy. Discover what temperature and humidity levels you are comfortable with and do not vary from those numbers when choosing where to go and when to go there. Use the special link titled "Climate Resources" on the Resources Page (http://www.vanabode.com/camp/links.htm) to find the expected temperatures and climate related information for millions of locations for each and every month of the year.

Some of our Destination Guide listings show the temperatures for the time of year we were there like this: 88/61. The first number is the hottest it got during the day Fahrenheit, and the second number is the coldest it got at night. So, in this case, you would be fine if these were numbers from a December day in Florida. The cool night means you sleep well and the air is dryer in the winter than the summer. The hotter day temperature means you can go swimming and beach hiking without having to wear coats or wetsuits.

All mobile societies from the original American Indians to modern day Himalayan Yak herders move their communities based on climate. When it gets cold they head south. When the spring comes they move north. Today, retirees called snowbirds migrate down from the north to stay in warm Florida during the winter. Many richer families have what they call a summer house and a winter house. You should strongly consider doing the same while Vanaboding. Just drive where the weather feels good.

You can estimate temperature changes using this formula. 1,000 feet of elevation = 3 degrees of temperature change. Example: In the summer if you drive UP 20-45 minutes into either Mount Charleston or Mount Potosi from Las Vegas, you will enjoy a perfect dry 72-76 degrees while Vegas is a boiling 100 degrees. Another example: spend the *summer* months in popular Flagstaff Arizona at 7,000 feet and enjoy nice 70-80 degree days and 50-60 degree nights then relocate a short 3-hour drive to Lake Havasu for the *winter*. At an elevation of only about 700 feet above sea level it is a nice temperature of about 65-82 degrees in the cold months and yet it is only 200 miles from Flagstaff. This strategy works better than driving 2,000 miles south for similar Florida temperatures in the winter.

Here are some overall recommendations concerning weather and temperatures. Avoid places that are colder than 40 degrees Fahrenheit at night. With a good sleeping bag or two as a blanket you will not be cold in any temperature above 30 degrees Fahrenheit while in bed. Obviously very cold weather or bundled sleeping will take some of the fun out of other activities.

Avoid any damp, muggy or humid states in the hot months: like Florida and Georgia, anywhere on either coast, or Southern California. In these wetter places you need a nighttime temperature that is not above 73 degrees. Sleeping at muggy temperatures much above 75 degrees at night is miserable. Your trip will suffer immeasurably.

In the dry areas like the West you can sleep well with nightly temperatures as high as 80 degrees. Without the humidity you can keep more ventilation going, your skin stays cooler and your bed stays dry. I was surprised to find this to be the case since I am a chronically hot sleeper.

Avoid dry places in the West when daytime temperatures go above 90 degrees. You cannot rest in the van during, say lunch, outdoor activities are not as fun, and the overall heat and sun drain you. You will be so tired that you want to take a short afternoon nap, but your bed will be too hot even in the shade. Also, cold food storage is a real drain on both your patience and your budget at these higher temperatures. If it gets hot enough you will spend $3 a day just on ice. Plus you have to burn fuel and drive to buy the ice, disrupting your daily plans, and that's *if* you can even find a store close by.

All the *Essentials of a Great Life* depend on good weather and climate. For example: *Good Personal Hygiene* is difficult to maintain if all you do is sweat day and night. *Healthy Sex* is impossible when you are suffering a heatstroke, shivering from the cold, or sticky from humidity. *Excellent Food* is hard to experience when it's too hot to cook or too cold to eat outside. *Great Sleep* is difficult in bad weather conditions and this severely affects everything else. You cannot *Prioritize Your Pleasure* when you are constantly fighting the elements.

As discussed in the other chapters you cannot neglect the proper treatment of these issues if you want to remain happy. This is true for everybody, everywhere, but especially true for travelers.

When it is too hot to sleep or have fun simply drive to a higher elevation or drive north.

It is more convenient, cheaper, easier, and faster to go up a few thousand feet in elevation than it is to drive thousands of miles to a more northerly location to get cooler weather. You can easily see temperatures nearly instantly using your smart phone and a free weather app. From there decide which nearby destination most closely matches your desired weather conditions.

Safety, Weapons, Security

I get more flak from misinformed readers and critics about personal security while van traveling than any other subject. I will spend a little energy in this chapter refuting those that say a van camping is dangerous.

Traveling and having a lot of fun can be just as safe as staying home, doing your normal daily chores, and living a typical boring life. For example; at home you may mow the grass, chop wood, repair an electrical outlet, cut an overhead tree branch, replace a shingle on the roof, overeat, exercise little, shovel snow from an icy driveway, and try to defend against thieves intent on robbing you of your household goods. While traveling in the van you will do none of this. Why? Because there is nearly nothing to repair or defend.

Thieves know there is not that much they can steal from a small vehicle, whereas a house has all sorts of valuable items of interest. This is why there are so many more house robberies than car break-ins. In 20+ years we have never been attacked, robbed or threatened while in the van or out hiking while Vanaboding.

Reference the **Sleep** chapter for information on choosing a safe and smart place to spend the night. Simply follow the same sensible strategies you follow when living out of a house and you will have less problems than ever. Don't do anything stupid like parking in a bad area of town or leaving the van unlocked in the wilderness. Practice common sense. Don't put a license plate or sticker on your van that contains your name or nickname. Lock the van just like you do when you leave your house and go to the grocery store.

Firearms are the greatest weapons of all, but they come with inherent risks. If you have children aboard I do not recommend their use under any circumstances. Each state has different laws concerning the transport of guns, especially across state lines and through border patrols. I sometimes carry a gun and keep it under the bed mattress fully loaded and ready to shoot while camping in some states or regions, especially out west. On the East Coast, forget about it. Guns are more trouble than they are worth.

I purchased J. Scott Kappas' fantastic reference book updated each year titled *Travelers guide to the firearms laws of the fifty states*. This book is a must have for anyone that is traveling *many* states with a firearm. Each state is carefully and individually addressed as to the most essential elements of carry laws like: felony possession, locked or unlocked carry case, automatic versus semi-automatic, firearm uniformity law, open carry, concealed carry, vehicle carry by permittees and non permittees, state parks, and the very important "duty to notify law enforcement officers of permit and carry status" law. He also breaks down the states into levels of total freedom versus total prohibition.

This book helped us decide to not carry our firearm during a special super low budget, 50 mile a day, east coast intensive city tour involving states like New York, the district of Washington DC and Illinois. Why? According to Kappas it seems there are many ways to commit a felony in these states with the improper handling of firearms. I think you would be an idiot to even consider transporting them unless you are a single woman. Typically the police seem to feel less threatened by females and firearms. Therefore they seem more tolerant.

I am interested in safe, fun, stress free travel. After working though his book it is clear that I will rely on other tools and strategies for staying safe. I will use common sense, stay alert, practice good parking strategies, carry my special highly recommended pepper blaster, and my Spyderco knife. The unique pepper spray product is shown in the EQUIPMENT portion of the Amazon Vanabode Store (http://www.vanabode.com/camp/amazon-travel-store.htm).

This has **NEVER** happened to us in over 700,000 miles of road travel over the course of 20+ years, but if it did, this is how I would handle it. Write these steps down on a piece of paper. Hang it where you can see it. Memorize it. 1) If someone tried to get in the van while I was sleeping in it, first, I would make sure they were not a police officer. 2) Then I would yell in a loud stern calm voice "back off or I will shoot you!" while honking the horn continuously. 3) If they continued to try to gain access I would start the van and drive away. I would not let them stop me from driving the van by standing in front of it. I would drive over them if they did that because that would mean there is a second party trying to gain access and they are just stalling me. 4) If all these tactics fail I would shoot through the roof once as a final warning (if carrying a gun). 5) If that failed to scare them off then I would fire upon anyone in sight to protect my person, family, and possessions.

I cannot offer you legal advice, but this is what I would do if anyone ever threatened me while in a vehicle, whether Vanaboding or not. I repeat though, we have had no such bad incidents in 20+ years of traveling the United States.

I keep a super high quality stainless steel military capable Spyderco knife latched to the wall of the van over the bed. This way I can grab it quickly if I ever need it. I carry a small portable highly specialized pepper spray weapon discussed above, whether in the van or hiking, as a deterrent to unwanted contact with person or animal. In some states pepper spray is considered a weapon so do not routinely carry it into normal public places like libraries, restaurants that serve liquor, government buildings, museums, and galleries.

Use a steering wheel lock commonly referred to as a "club" to lock the steering column when not in the van. Criminals have indicated that both dogs and steering wheel locks do deter them. Keep all doors and windows locked and rolled up all the way. Always use the windshield cover. Put up the curtains to block anyone's view of the interior whether you are in the van or not.

Keep a cell phone charged and turned on. If parking street side or near a business ALWAYS note your location *before going to sleep*. If you ever have to call for help you want to be able to quickly tell the dispatcher exactly where you are, even if you have to give GPS coordinates rather than an address or street intersection. If you just pull in, and park in the dark, how will you tell emergency staff where you are if you need them?

Almost every single car break in is done by a petty criminal looking to steal the sound system or any loose belongings, and make a quick, conflict free escape. The fact that you are inside the vehicle will deter anyone of this type from continuing any kind of illegal activity. Simply let them know you are there. Car jacking's get a lot of media attention. They are extremely rare though and when they do happen they are usually associated with drug activity in dangerous inner city areas. Never go to these kind of places. Using your van as a Vanabode will not make you any more susceptible to car jacking's.

Vanaboding is far safer overall than staying home and trying to defend yourself and house and car from criminals. The transient nature of traveling makes it even more difficult for people to target you because for one: they see you have nothing to steal, and two; you are gone by the time anybody that cares is around. To further make my point; I have owned houses, townhomes and condos over the course of my life; and had over $65,000 in damage done to them in 20 years from natural disasters and thieves breaking in while I was gone. By contrast I have not lost a single item while Vanaboding.

The **Inventory** chapter lists safety gear to use while on the road.

What is Stopping You?

What do you do if you have no time for yourself? Get rid of *time* constraints by getting rid of your job. Get rid of your *job* by getting rid of your debt. Get rid of your *debt* by not buying things you don't need. Stop buying things you don't need when you have the *time* to have more fun without them. Problem solved. Period. Done.

Do you have what you think are one hundred other reasons why you can't do what you want to do? Read on for the practical step-by-step plans to getting what you want out of life including how to address school, work, money, debt and your leisure time. When you are finished with this book you will be able to develop a solid strategy that will work for you. If you want to Vanabode you need a plan to get debt free now and support yourself while traveling the country.

The four biggest reasons most people give for never traveling and living their dreams are *debt, children, possessions, and fear*. I will show you how to either eliminate these; or travel and live in spite of these additional challenges. The following text covers the most common issues separating people from their dreams and preventing them from having fun along with a sensible, achievable means by which to overcome each problem. Scan down and find your situation and your solution.

DEBT stops more people from doing what they really want with their lives than any other element. Greed and peer pressure influences us to buy stuff we don't need. Then we spend years working to pay for it. Often these years are not fun ones. These lost years create resentment and overwhelm us with disappointment. If you are deep in debt or locked upside down in a 30-year mortgage I recommend you read and reread the **Budget** chapter.

I am in my late 40's and have a much greater understanding of time than most people. Many may not grasp what I am saying here but it is extremely important that you work with this until it is clear. Your life: *which is your time*, depends on it. The simple truth: *It is not money you are short of, but time.*

If you spend your whole life working to pay off debts then what have you lived for? Take your life, *your time*, and enjoy it *now*. You cannot prioritize your pleasure if you are deeply in debt. There are a number of ways to get out of debt. I obviously do not know your exact situation but these three strategies will be helpful to most people.

Debt Solution #1 - sell what you don't need, pay off your debts, and travel on the remaining proceeds. This is the simplest path if you are *not* in dire circumstances, but just struggling with a boring life of making money and paying bills: going nowhere and doing nothing. To preserve your credit avoid filing bankruptcy or skipping out on paying your debts.

First use the **Budget** chapter to figure out the spending range you want to be in. Then decide how much money you need in the bank to Vanabode for the length of time you want to be out. Example: if you decide to Vanabode on $30 a day and want to be out for 9 months you need about $8,100 in the bank. Of course if you are making money while on the road like I do (http://www.vanabode.com/camp/quit-your-job-make-money.htm) or you have a steady income from say a rental investment, savings interest, or retirement income, then you won't need as much saved in order to take off.

Now, sell everything you do not need to get you the $8,100 for your nine-month adventure. Buy the Van. Sell everything else that is not going with you. When my wife and I first took off we sold every stick of furniture we had. We sold all our appliances, clothes, cars, motorcycles, yard equipment, and junk. We put a few things like photo albums and keepsake gifts from dead relatives at our mother's houses and in a small storage unit. Later we even closed the storage unit too. This is how you become free. Don't fret about it. Just sell it all. If you have some real special valuables or something of sentimental value that you do not think you can part with: weigh the cost of storing it at a storage facility to the cost of simply replacing it later with the cash you save *by not storing it*.

Keep your current job and live on $600 a month in your Vanabode until you have the full $8,100 or more saved. Then leave, travel and enjoy yourself. Locate jobs for traveling campers just like yourself to refill your pocket book using the resources on the make money page (http://www.vanabode.com/camp/quit-your-job-make-money.htm).

Debt Solution #2 - bankruptcy is the last resort for the truly desperate. If you are completely overwhelmed, upside down, and losing everything anyway, you *can* file bankruptcy. You will basically sell everything from clothes to cars that you do not need to Vanabode and spend the cash on purchasing all the items shown in the **Inventory** chapter. Then you are set to live comfortably regardless of how the bankruptcy proceedings go. Do NOT do this lightly.

Most any person or company can file for bankruptcy protection. But simply filing is not the goal. The goal is to remove all debt while leaving you with everything you need to travel or live a long time through Vanaboding. You must have a serious plan in place in order to pull this off. You MUST use a professional bankruptcy attorney to walk you through this, as the courts will not just let you keep what you want. Each state operates under different rules even though our bankruptcy laws are federal.

The best resource if you are very serious about getting absolute top level advice from a real professional is Privacy Crisis (http://www.vanabode.com/camp/hide-your-money-privacy.htm) which shows you how to protect your assets, disappear, escape from government intrusion, eliminate debt, stop wage garnishment, bank secretly, escape stalkers and much more. It also shows you how and where to literally store and conceal cash and valuables in a secure lock down facility safe box *without revealing your identity:* which is absolutely critical. This book could actually save your life (your time) and help make your transition to freedom successful.

Many people do not file bankruptcy. They just drop everything they are doing and simply walk away and never pay the debts they owe. Some take whatever they have, pay off the van, prepay the insurance and other bills like cell phone contracts or mail service for a year in advance and hit the road. Bill collectors can't do much to you if you don't have anything for them to take or a place for them to mail the collection notices to.

Debt Solution #3 - if you cannot or will not get out of debt in 2 years or less then consider Vanaboding only a week at a time. This way you can keep your job and chip away at your debts. You will never experience true freedom this way, still tethered to your job, creditors, and daily expenses, but you can have *some* fun. This will demonstrate how important all the issues in this book are to your ultimate freedom. The more of your life you get back the more you will want back, as new experiences become a big motivator for you.

Vanaboding *part time to start with* may be enough to help you break out of what you have been stuck in so long. Consider the part time money making strategies while you keep your day job on the make money page (http://www.vanabode.com/camp/quit-your-job-make-money.htm). I worked for NASA full time and wrote simple web sites part time at night until my part time income exceeded my NASA income. Then I sold everything, quit the job and hit the road.

Under this plan the first step is to trade your vehicle for the van described in the **Van** chapter and properly outfit it. This won't cost any more than having a typical car or sport utility vehicle. Try out some short cheap trips while paying down your debt. Sell everything you do not need, move into a smaller cheaper house, or better yet move into your van and start testing out the logistics of the Vanabode. Eat out less. Cancel all nonessential expenditures except those associated with Vanaboding. Then travel longer and further as you pay off your debts a little at a time.

An empty savings account is a form of indebtedness. This is why employers pay you just enough to keep you working, but not enough that you can save money and get ahead. They know if they let you get ahead by saving money you won't need them anymore. You won't be *indebted*. They want to keep you and the profits you provide so they limit the amount they pay you. Do not let a zero balance in your savings account prevent you from escaping the rat race and really enjoying yourself for a decent length of time. Resist this.

When I took my first long 9 month trip over 15 years ago I paid for the entire thing with a pair of credit cards. I had no money saved. I kept the expenditures very low. I stayed free in super cool places for weeks at a time rather than driving thousands of miles every month. We spent very little dining out.

You can do the same thing we did. Use a credit card or personal loan to get started, then pay it back later. People take out loans for things that bring them far less pleasure than an extended life-changing trip around the country. Be careful though. Do not go into debt you cannot repay.

We came back from the 9 month trip with no regrets. My wife and I had an extraordinary time. It opened my eyes. Now I was very motivated to figure out how to do this forever. We got new jobs, paid off the credit cards and lived the Vanabode lifestyle part-time. I worked for NASA and my wife worked as a medical transcriptionist and fitness instructor.

Then we realized if we wanted to travel more we would need to reduce our overhead. We sold everything and moved into a small motorhome. We were able to keep normal high paying jobs while reducing our overhead to a minimum. As far as I know I was the only person out of thousands working at the massive prestigious NASA headquarters in Cape Canaveral, Florida that was living in an RV. But I had a goal in mind and I was not going to give up.

Time restrictions are an extension of the debt issues excuse. When you ask people why they are not doing the things in their life that they want to do, they invariably answer "I don't have the time". What they are really saying is *they don't have the means to leave their current income stream* that would free up the time they need. For example If I GAVE most working class Americans an airplane ticket to France and a paid up hotel room for one month MOST of them would still not be able to go and stay the entire month. These worker bees will probably not have a full month to themselves until they are in a retirement home. Game over. Vanabode empowers you to reclaim your life by lowering your overhead thus eliminating your indebtedness to the world's time and money system.

Kids present a unique situation. Do not attempt the *strict* Vanabode lifestyle if you have more than two people in your party. There is not enough room or privacy for more than two in a van. If you have lots of kids like I do, you need to modify my strategies in this book to suit the number of people in your party. I have three children and they were young when I first started this. I was somewhat limited in my approach to long term travel and living abroad because of my lovely little ones. I overcame the difficulties because I wanted it badly.

I sold my house and purchased a large RV. We went on some very long trips using this Class A motorhome with sleeping areas for six people. By using the large RV instead of the van we were able to comfortably take the kids along. But it came at a cost. We were unable to stay in big cities like San Francisco or Las Vegas for long. We were limited in the length of time we could spend in National Parks as well. They have limited spots for large motorhomes to stay long term. Operating from a motorhome is considerably more expensive than strict Vanaboding. With children, it is a necessary expense though, so budget for it.

Most young children love to travel. Once they are out there with you exploring and seeing new things every day, you will probably never hear a single lifestyle related complaint. Pay extra attention to the safety issues covered in the **Security** chapter when you have kids aboard. Address the child's education plan before leaving. In most states it is illegal for a child to be out of school if he or she is under 16 years old. But there is an elegant, solid solution to this problem.

Children can be legally home schooled using the resources of hundreds of innovative online educational companies all over the world. My kids were home schooled for years. The home schooling system has proven time and time again to be far superior to our public school system in the developing of intelligence, workplace skills, and social and emotional well-being.

If your child is getting into trouble, drugs, premarital sex, violence, gangs, or just not learning, then I highly recommend you take a year or more and Vanabode. *There is no substitute* for getting them away from all these pressures that thrive in the public school system. Get them out where they can experience the real world *with you*. This will be the greatest educational experience your child will ever have. Keep them out until they mature enough to handle peer pressure, until they are ready to be an adult. Make the journey and lifestyle change a joy, not a punishment. Society has probably convinced you that childhood is for school. That is a lie.

Children can be a powerful reason to take a serious long trip around the U.S. Name a gift you give a child, or any age person for that matter, that will be more appreciated for the rest of their lives than a great trip filled with mind-blowing adventure and thrilling memories? I have never met anyone that regretted the time they spent showing someone the world. I have never met anyone that regretted taking one of these trips as a child. Conventional schooling cannot match it.

Possessions are a big problem in America. Consumerism and greed seem real cool when you are watching some television show about how a super star or famous actor lives in this big mansion, throwing big parties all the time and living large. But it is all a lie. Nearly every person I've ever met has suffered from *possession overload*. (http://www.vanabode.com/jason-terms.htm) The more they own the more they can't use what they own. Why? Because they underestimate the time it takes to pay for the toy, to insure it, and protect it, and repair it, and fuel it up, and get it licensed, and on and on.

Take boats for example. Except for those rare individuals who are smart enough to live on or work from their boat, nearly everyone else hardly ever uses their boat. Florida is the boat capital of the world. I have spent at least 30 years of my life here off and on. You can go to any Florida boat yard and marina and see hundreds of boats, cruisers, and yachts sitting dry-docked in the yard. They need repair, they cost money to insure, and they cost money to store. They are depreciating and wearing out and they aren't even being used! Obviously the folks that spent hundreds of thousands of dollars on these boats are absolutely sick at where they end up.

Fear is one of the most limiting powers on Earth. It is good in certain situations, but to experience romance and adventure, you have to feel it, then nullify it. For example, I will gladly embrace a chest full of fear and back off when I see a massive grizzly bear and cub when hiking Glacier National Park (http://www.rvforsaleguide.com/glacier-national-park.htm) But I *don't let fear of bears keep me out of the park altogether*. See the difference?

If you really want to get out and change your life the very first thing you need to do is identify what is stopping you. If it is not debt, kids, or possessions then you have it easy. Why? Because just about the only thing left to overcome is fear. Since fear is often nothing more than a negative artificial reaction to an unlikely event, *you can overcome it!* Unlike being in debt, you don't have to change your entire economic situation. Unlike large families you, don't have to overcome the schooling issue or travel in a larger vehicle. Simply overcome fear with a little planning and knowledge.

Analyze the alternative (http://www.vanabode.com/jason-terms.htm). One of the best ways I have developed for overcoming fear is to *take an intelligent honest look at the alternatives!* Identify what you are afraid of, then see what the alternatives are. Example: You are afraid that if you leave your house and go camping in your van, someone will break into your van and steal something. So the alternative is staying home right? Wrong! Someone can still steal from you. Now they can break into your house **and** your vehicle and steal something. You have a whole lot more to lose out of a house than you do out of a van. Travel like I advise and you won't have more than $900 worth of items with you. Besides who is going to steal your portable toilet, or your mattress, or your clothes, or a $3 bottle of propane?

We have traveled over 700,000 miles in 20 plus years and we have never had anything stolen out of our vehicles except $300 worth of jewelry once (we had a motor home *stored* in a business parking lot while we were gone working on a special assignment for 6 weeks.) *So, your fear of theft should be greater staying home than traveling!* By traveling we have already eliminated most thief's targets. We sold the junk he would have stolen from us and levered the proceeds to finance our journeys. So *analyze the alternative* to NOT traveling, and eliminated your misguided fear of theft with knowledge and understanding.

Another example: people fear not having enough money to take care of themselves when they get old so they hole up in a house and work their butt off trying to save a lot of money. Guess what? You probably won't have enough money to take care of yourself when you get old whether you stay home or not! Here's how it breaks down. *Analyze the alternative* to taking a chunk of savings and living it up for a year. Compare Vanaboding to huddling up in your house. As I demonstrate in the **Budget** chapter *you will spend more money living at home* than you do Vanaboding! That's a fact! The reality is you can live longer more happily while on a well-planned Vanabode trip than you can by any other method. So you can throw discard that misinformed plan of holing up in your house your entire life to save money for retirement. Why? Because you analyzed the alternative and you can actually save MORE money traveling in a Vanabode.

Theft and running out of savings are just two in a long list of things people fear. I can't give examples of how to overcome every single one of them but if you use my *analyze the alternative* approach to facing fear, you may find that you have more to fear *not* Vanaboding than you do embracing this adventure.

Sick family members usually fall into the fear category as well. Most people are afraid to take their loved one from familiar surroundings because they think they will suffer. Most times this is not true. Usually the terminally ill be more than happy to get out and handle the extra difficulties involved in traveling. They do it gladly in exchange for living a little; seeing a new incredible place they have always dreamed of, or making lasting memories with their family. Just ask them.

If you or your loved one is very ill, especially with a life threatening and terminal illness, then you have many serious decisions to make. Sitting home and doing nothing is usually the most unrewarding of your choices. If the sick person knows they will die soon, you need to discuss this with them and determine what they want to do or experience before they pass away. Ask yourself, *"If I only had a little time left to live, what would I want to do?"*

The truth is, regardless of how healthy you are; regardless of how much money you have; and in spite of how young you may see yourself; you do not have much time left either. Neither do I. I have never met an older person that did not regret *not* traveling, living, loving, and doing more when they had the chance. Vanaboding gives nearly everyone the chance to live a dream. Take it.

Daniel Suelo graduated from the University of Colorado in 1987 with a degree in Anthropology. He made plenty of money as he held typical jobs after leaving school. However, like so many, he discovered there was something missing in his life. So he decided to do something extraordinary. Daniel did not let anything stop him. He escaped from debt and tiresome worthless tasks to a level that even I cannot match.

Since 2000, Daniel Suelo has called a cave, one hour walking distance from Moab, his home. I've been there and it's beautiful. Like the guy in the brilliant movie *Office Space* he decided he didn't like paying bills or working so he just quit going to work and he just quit paying bills. He also decided to stop using money altogether. Period. He goes to the public library to maintain his blog, which doesn't cost him a penny. According to Daniel Suelo's blog, he doesn't ask for any government assistance and never uses food stamps or money in order to survive.

He collects food from the riverbank and forest for food. He collects items others have discarded to enhance his daily life. Sounds hard, but remember this guy never has to report for work, pay taxes or bills, or waste time with hundreds of other life sapping chores. He appears in great shape and claims he has never gone hungry. I consider Vanaboding a nice compromise between living like I used to live and living in a cave like Daniel has.

If you just need money to travel on then see the working from home resources. (http://www.vanabode.com/camp/quit-your-job-make-money.htm). In summary identify what is stopping you, then use the action plans above to overcome the situation. If you need help with a unique set of circumstances contact me (http://www.vanabode.com/contact.htm). I will be glad to help. You may also post your story on the Vanabode Forum to get help from others as well as myself (http://forums.vanabode.com).

How to Disappear

I did not write this book with this subject in mind. However many readers and customers have shown a lot of interest in disappearing, in starting over, in getting off the grid, in identity theft prevention measures, and in escaping stalkers. This page will give you a quick overview of how to do it. However, *if you are really serious* about this subject you MUST visit these two pages on the Vanabode website: Protect your identity, location, privacy and money (http://www.vanabode.com/camp/hide-your-money-privacy.htm) and Escape a Stalker in 12 hours (http://www.vanabode.com/camp/escape-stalker.htm).

Essentially anytime you place your name or social security number on a document or allow someone to put them into a database you immediately become exploitable and findable. The only perfect strategy for totally disappearing is to start a new life where you never do that again. Do not sign for a mortgage or rental agreement. Do not authorize a background check. Do not allow anyone to run a credit report run on you. If you want to be invisible and live so nobody can find you: stalkers, nasty enemies, rude or destructive family members, creditors, etc., then you need to be able to travel and live without signing on the dotted line for anybody.

Set up a corporation, small business, trust, or other legal holding company that hides *your* name from the public. Then purchase your van in this new holding companies name, *not* your name. Only the holding company's information is on the vehicle registration, license plate and title. It is owned by the holding company (you are just taking care of the paperwork for the company).

You can take this further by getting credit cards in the holding companies name as well so you can pay for things that way. Alternatively you could simply pay cash for everything. There are strategies dealing with all the other issues as well in the book, like how to get mail, when to show your real driver's license, how to avoid giving a real name when visiting a campground, how to rent without revealing your identity, etc. This process is involved but many different people do it every day for many different reasons. *If you are really serious* about this subject you must visit the web pages shown above about Grant Hall's information.

The bottom line is if you Vanabode you can lead a great life even though you may find yourself in unique circumstances that require you to go off the grid for a while. You are not alone. Use this book and the ones recommended above, to own and control your new identity, time, and life.

Pay Pal founder and early Facebook investor Peter Thiel gave $1.25 million towards the creation of a floating libertarian country in international waters. The idea is to create a new country starting without typical existing laws and rules or moral codes and allowing each person to obtain complete personal anonymity. This new country will be built on a giant floating barge. They think it will be a place that no other country can lord over. If *you* want to disappear, eliminate stress, be free, and remove yourself from most of the confining laws in our society, you don't have to spend billions building an offshore entity, simply Vanabode.

Making Money While Traveling

While Vanaboding you do not have to make a lot of money in order to do a lot. Rather, you can *do a lot with very little money*. This lifestyle is about reducing costs and enhancing your life by spending **time** *living* a fun life rather than spending **money** *trying to buy* a fun life. It is not about attending college, pursuing a career, or earning $200,000 a year. Still, even though you don't need much money to Vanabode successfully, you will need some money.

Henry David Thoreau said in his 1854 release of *Walden* ...a strolling Indian went to sell baskets at the house of a well-known lawyer in my neighborhood. "Do you wish to buy any baskets?" he asked. "No, we do not want any," was the reply. "What!" exclaimed the Indian as he went out the gate, "do you mean to starve us?" Having seen his industrious white neighbors so well off (that the lawyer had only to weave arguments, and, by some magic, wealth and standing followed) he had said to himself: I will go into business; I will weave baskets; it is a thing, which I can do. Thinking that when he had made the baskets he would have done his part, and then it would be the white man's (responsibility) to buy them. He had not discovered that it was necessary for him to make it worth the others while to buy them, or at least make him think that it was so, or to make something else which it would be worth his while to buy. I too had woven a kind of basket of a delicate texture, but I had not made it worth any one's while to buy it. Yet not the less, in my case, did I think it worth my while to weave them, and ***instead of studying how to make it worth men's while to buy my baskets, I studied rather how to avoid the necessity of selling them.***"

This is brilliant math. This is beautiful simplicity. Why study, then work, so you can make something to possibly sell, to earn money, to buy something you don't need? Why not instead study how to live happily without that something others are working their entire lives to get? This is one of the reasons why van dwelling; and Vanaboding for those that want to travel many miles a year, works so well.

This lifestyle eliminates unneeded consumption, waste, work, taxation, and employment that often lead to near enslavement. Instead of figuring out how to make tons of money, you figure out what you really need, and obtain that *without* the unnecessary 40 hour a week job. Do you really want to pursue money and things via a college education, and then follow it up with 30 years at a job you don't like?

As Michael Bunker pointed out in his book *Surviving Off Off-Grid*: "The world system needs eaters and buyers, so it creates and trains them. Colonizing and training minds is the ultimate purpose behind public education." Remember most institutions are designed to make you NEED what it is they are selling. With a new philosophy and a Vanabode you can circumvent this entire sinkhole. Use the $100,000 educational experience they are trying to sell you in the form of a diploma as kindling for your camp fire.

Millions all over the world suit up daily to do the most unfulfilling, de-humanizing, useless work, and then tell me they cannot travel because they have no time! What? What are you even saying? What are you working for if you have no TIME when you are done? Money, you answer? Guess what. Money is USELESS without time!

In 300 years this beautiful country of people has gone from intelligent interesting brave explorers to pathetic consumer slaves, pitiful fat eaters and drinkers, doing it all for their new lords, the very rich and powerful politically connected. As a proud American it can be embarrassing. When we visit the National Parks there is usually what appears to be less than

30% able-bodied U.S. citizens there. The other 70% or so appear to be foreigners on vacation (Europeans get 2-3 months off work every year), or retired folks that are so old they cannot walk any trail or path longer than one-quarter mile and do not see anything except what is pointed out to them from the bus window. When I ask people why they do not visit a national park they all say the same thing, "We don't have time."

Of course, you can easily afford to Vanabode forever if you have a pension, investment income, savings, Social Security income, rental income, or disability check. Some people work half a year in the far north where the jobs are only open seasonally. Then they collect unemployment compensation and live off that for the rest of the year. Each state operates differently so check this option carefully before depending on it. You can make things and sell them on the Internet or earn money repairing stuff.

You can probably travel the rest of your life by simply selling everything you already own and buying a van and outfitting it from the proceeds. If you *don't* already have income or savings here's my initial list of some ways to earn money while traveling all over the country. You can travel forever if you want to by employing any of these options. Some people go on short trips using our strategies and keep up a house and normal job. Some people simply travel on savings, retirement benefits, or other passive income and when they run out of money stop somewhere nice, and work any kind of job until their savings are replenished. I am married and when I first started traveling heavily, I also had three kids to take care of. Since I Vanabode for months and sometimes years at a time I need a more steady income.

The following is just a partial list, without much detail, to whet your appetite. If you are ready to get started making money right now, I have **MUCH** more information on these methods on the make money page (http://www.vanabode.com/camp/quit-your-job-make-money.htm) on the Vanabode website. There I include special links to the companies that will pay you and links to important business connections that few know of. Do this before leaving on long Vanabode trips so you don't feel stressed and you can really relax and enjoy yourself.

Internet web site owner - write articles to be published on the Internet, own and manage your own website, blog, forum or travel diary. I have been making a good living doing this since 2004. Anyone can do it. No experience is required, but you must be able to type, copy and paste, and follow written instructions.

Work at campgrounds in areas you want to visit. The make money page (http://www.vanabode.com/camp/quit-your-job-make-money.htm) lists sites with 1,000's of camping jobs including free campsites in National Parks, in all 50 states, for all ages.

Run a food concession trailer or pull a hotdog cart and make money cheaply.

Sell an Ebook just like the one you are reading right now. Nearly any subject can be profitably written about, and you don't have to be an English major to write one.

Write books, short stories, and more and earn money from any location.

Entertainers like magicians, mentalists, jugglers, clowns, musicians and others can earn money while mobile.

Write a movie script and earn money selling your film ideas to Hollywood.

Stock trading with specialized trading tools can make you a lot of money. Learn how to use the Automated Forex Trading System. There is some risk involved in this one as with any free market investment. Be smart.

Get paid for your feedback previewing movie trailers, filling out questionnaires, taking surveys, doing reviews, and providing consumer opinions of products.

eBay makes it possible to sell anything while Vanaboding. Others ship it for you, all you do is oversee customer service by answering customer's questions via email.

Freelance work online, write, type, proofread, consult, program, promote, blog, review, and more for money. I show you where to apply and post your profile for free.

Consulting businesses are easy to run, people pay for whatever specialized skills or knowledge you have that they need.

I will pay you to write about your Vanabode trips and experiences using my simple Word template contact me (http://www.vanabode.com/contact.htm).

Forums and Blogs need someone to oversee them, remove Spam, answer questions, and work comments.

Estate sitters take care of rich people's houses while they are away, protect them, clean them, earn a salary, and live rent free.

Vending truck/trailer enables you to sell food, drinks, gifts, specialty items, and crafts, from your van or trailer.

Write songs placing your work on major music stores, like iTunes, Sony, Yahoo.

If you don't have savings visit my earning a living page on the Internet. (http://www.vanabode.com/camp/quit-your-job-make-money.htm). **This page has all the links to the above sources for jobs, work and income.**

Inventory

Use this list to keep your traveling cheap, fun, and hassle free. Power Inverters allow you to run normal household equipment from your vans power source, the battery. You can run a small hairdryer, charge your cell phone, power a small electric skillet or cooking element, recharge your camera and computer batteries, hook up a low voltage 12 volt cooler, power a small fan, power a light, and most anything else that has a normal household plug. Make sure you get a higher wattage one that accepts 2 plugs so you can power one thing while simultaneously recharging the battery on another. Buy one that has a built in fan to cool it, otherwise it will burn up in six months. Make sure it has an automatic low battery shutdown. This prevents discharging your van battery to the point you can't start the van.

We hooked the inverter straight into the 12-volt accessory receptacle that comes as an option on our van. This is NOT the same as a cigarette lighter power receptacle even though the plug receptacle may look the same. Cigarette lighter power outlets won't usually work long term for much of anything. Click the special discounted Camping World link I have set up for you on the Equipment Page (http://www.vanabode.com/camp/links.htm) online to purchase a well-made heavy-duty inverter.

I get a lot of criticism for not including solar power, gas heat, and electrical storage via batteries in my book. I don't include them for very good reasons. I don't need them. They are expensive. They take up a lot of room. They are dangerous. They are expensive and unreliable. They require a moderate to high level of technical skills to operate. They destroy your ability to stealth camp, thus raising your costs even further. They are thief magnets. Solar power is not the solution to generating energy for a mobile traveler who wants to move around effortlessly and stay virtually anywhere without cost.

If you are parked in the same spot for 6 months or longer you *might be able to come close* to justifying the use, cost and hassle of any of these. The pure Vanabode strategies I outline in this book make these systems nearly obsolete. They are called SYSTEMS for a reason. The system only works if every single complicated expensive part of it works properly. If just one small portion is not working correctly, just one loose wire, or just one messed up diode hidden beneath some complicated circuit board, and all you have is a pile of heavy, space stealing junk, just itching to draw the attention of some wandering thief. Take a look at this unbelievable image of a solar charging and storage system wiring diagram and you will see why I just walk around this problem. (http://www.vanabode.com/camp/solar-

charging-system.htm).

A thermometer with reliable *indoor and outdoor* readings makes planning what to wear on your days and nights easier. You don't want to crawl out of the van in a t-shirt only to find it is 20 degrees outside. These also help you know how long you can stay out hiking and how much water to take with you. Knowing the temperature will help you decide how long you can safely leave your pet in the vehicle with only the roof vent open and how much ice to purchase. They help you decide if you want to continue staying in a particular location. If it gets one degree hotter each night and two degrees hotter each day you may start planning to move to a higher elevation to stay cool.

Ours has a maximum and minimum setting which shows the hottest and coldest temperatures for the previous 24 hours. We installed it in 5 minutes without modifying the van. We ran the outdoor sensor, which is nothing more than a thin wire, through the door where it closes against the rubber molding. You can find them at automotive stores and Walmart.

Mirrors make keeping your good face on much easier. When you are camping and skipping showers every now and then a small hand mirror will help you stay looking your best. If you go on a long hikes or sleep outdoors use the mirror to check areas of your body you can't see without it for biting and invasive insects like ticks. Mirrors can be used in emergencies to signal for help. I use one for shaving if I am out in a remote area. If you see

fluid leaking from under your van use the mirror to more easily locate its source.

Roof vents are a specialty item that not every person will want or need. We had ours installed at a motorhome dealership and wired directly to the van's standard 12 volt system. Parts and labor cost $320. This allows us to ventilate the van without the key being in the van ignition for up to 10 continuous hours. *Make sure and have it installed facing backwards*, so the wind won't rip it off the roof the first time you drive away and accidentally leave it up. Make sure it has a multi-speed fan so you can easily manage temperature and humidity. Get one with a screen to keep insects out. You will be using it often.

These vents make it easy to stay cool night and day. They keep your pets happier.

They help maintain the security of your vehicle. They help whether you are away or asleep, because you need not open any other windows to get fresh air.

Do not install a *cheap* roof vent or you will be sorry. You don't want anything to fail, especially on the roof of your home, which would allow wind, rain, mildew, trash, bugs, or other elements in. If you install one, choose one from a name brand manufacturer with a higher amperage motor, with a heavy plastic vent cover, and a very small profile so it doesn't reveal the fact that you are camping in the van. I recommend the Fan-Tastic brand of vent with the lowest profile and a manual crank. You can find a link to it in the EQUIPMENT part Vanabode Store (http://www.vanabode.com/camp/amazon-travel-store.htm). Unless you are going to be in the snow a lot get the white on white one. The black one gets hot.

The picture shows the vent in the raised position with the fan running to pull cool air inside and expel hot air. Do not buy one that sticks up above the roof of the van more than a couple of inches when in its *lowered* position because that will reveal that you are camping and sleeping inside. See the first picture in this book that shows what the low profile vent looks like in the lowered position.

Never take a chance on smashing or cracking the fragile plastic lid by driving through low hanging trees. Water coming in the roof of your vehicle will ruin everything. Do not mount it directly over the bed. Purchase high quality components and have a professional handle the installation. I keep a spare cover under the wheel well storage under the bed. This is not the actual vent, but the plastic cover only. If it ever breaks while on the road it could take up to a week to get one shipped so I like keeping a spare. Handle the roof vent issue right or don't do it at all. This is important.

Clothes are normally about personal style but they take on a much greater importance when traveling. Take only one set of upscale dress clothes. Rarely will you need anything more than clean casual attire. Take one pair of dress shoes, one pair of hiking or sports shoes, and as many pairs of sandals as you can carry. Sandals eliminate smelly feet, take up less room, and help reduce laundry volume because you aren't washing smelly socks. Sandals are cheap, and make it easy to wash your feet when in a public bathroom.

Great *sleeping* temperatures range from 40 to 72 degrees at night. This means the *day* temperatures are usually warmer than 70 degrees so large heavy coats are not needed. Multiple layers of comfortable long sleeve tee shirts and sweaters with a light windbreaker jacket will be easier to manage, be easier to pack, and be more comfortable. Obviously when you are inside sleeping in a warm bed covered with a soft sleeping bag you don't need clothes. When outside though carry a warm hat that covers the ears and comfortable gloves. These take up little room while affording you a lot of warmth and wind protection. The single most important clothing item is a good quality, flexible, medium to wide brim hat for sun protection. Buy one and wear it whether you like hats or not.

Sun protection will become a big issue when you are away from the office for 6 months. Tan legs cover cellulite but you won't care how great your legs look if your nose is rotting off from skin cancer. I have already had surgery on my face a few times due to skin cancer that probably got started from surfing Florida for years unprotected. Hats also improve your appearance when you haven't washed your hair in 3 days.

The picture shows the fisherman's pocket vest that I wear when hiking or going into a retail store to clean up using public bathrooms. I keep the pockets preloaded with all the toiletries I need to carry in to the store like a toothbrush, toothpaste, shampoo, soap, razor,

dental floss, nail clippers, tweezers, and more. I keep the vest hanging in the van, grab it and go.

I also highly recommend a loose, lightweight, white, long sleeve shirt used by outdoors enthusiasts to protect from the sun and wick away moisture. You can wear it all day and skip putting tons of sun block or bug repellent on that part of your body. Then when you are done, simply soak it in a small bit of water, wring it out, and hang it to dry. It will be ready to wear the next day.

Bring single layer nylon surf-type swimsuits and surfer style single pocket shorts. Cotton is a very poor choice whereas nylons and synthetics dry quickly. States like California, Florida, and others out west have warm water lakes, rivers, ponds, and other bodies of water you can easily get clean in. You can swim bathe using a biodegradable earth friendly soap. Simply reach in your loose fitting clothes, wash your hidden regions by hand, then go under the water and rinse off. When you are done get out and drip dry. Within an hour or two your clothes are not only dry but clean too. This eliminates frequent laundry facility trips increasing the fun factor.

Capture great memories cheaply with a digital camera. Buy a small one with a simple protective case big enough to carry 4-6 back up batteries. Make sure it has a minimum of 3 mega pixels for quality. Get the lightest one you can afford with a USB port or other means of transferring to a computer. Most importantly it needs a good battery management system including a car charger, and a normal prong plug household charger so you can charge up 4 to 8 batteries at a time. If you take lots of pictures for weeks on end, you will need several external digital cards to swap out when one gets full. Don't get a camera with less than ten times *optical* zoom (not digital zoom which is grossly inferior).

When you are out for a while taking hundreds of pictures you don't want to hassle with your camera. You want the picture taking to be part of the experience; but not prevent you from being *present* in the very spot you are photographing. You don't want a camera that you have to hassle with, that stops you from taking in the smells, the sounds, the tastes, the colors, and everything else the camera cannot capture.

These pictures will serve to remind you of the experiences you have had. They can bring back the memory of some fantastic moment, like the hug you shared with your lover on the cliffs edge on a foggy cool morning in La Jolla, or the bright yellow eyes of the coyote outside Death Valley just before sunset. If all you can remember when you look at the pictures later is "oh yea we went there" then you are missing the very point of travel. I call it Romance Wasting (http://www.vanabode.com/jason-terms.htm).

My strategy works like this: first I shoot pictures, and then using a USB connection, I transfer them to my computer. Then I burn them onto CD's and store them elsewhere in the van as a backup in case the computer goes down or is stolen. Then I empty the digital camera cards and reuse them to shoot more pictures. You can also take the USB cards or CD's into any photo lab and have prints made from them. You can upload the pictures to a free online photographic storage site as a backup. Make sure when you upload your photos that you are storing the original high resolution version and not some reduced quality version for online viewing only.

DVD recorders make shooting adventure movies fun. The smaller ones are better for travel. You need a good 10X *optical* zoom minimum. I like the kind that burns directly onto mini DVD's as they are the easiest to use. However, most people prefer pure digital cameras so they can make the movie and instantly upload it to the web or YouTube for safekeeping. The battery life and the charging system are important as described in the digital camera section above. The biggest weakness of most cameras is they handle poor light badly. Get one that specifically mentions good light handling ability, as you will be shooting in extreme and varied conditions. Practice using the camera often.

It is important to correctly handle storage issues when traveling in a small vehicle. Every storage solution should be light, easy to get to, and secure enough to handle the motion of a moving vehicle. I prefer clear plastic heavy-duty containers with lids measured and fitted so as to not waste space in my van, coupled with bungee cords. Storage needs change depending on the trip, weather, geography and any extra toys that each particular area may call for. Leave some space empty to accommodate that bottle of wine you plan to drink the next day, or that gallon basket of fresh organic blueberries you bought at the Sausalito Farmers Market, or the firewood you plan to burn next week, or the boogie board you will use on this particular beach trip only. Don't fill every square foot of space.

You don't want to spend two minutes rummaging through the back door access in a dust storm looking in a shirt container to find a can of beans. Keep what you use often up front. Clear containers work because you can see what you need quickly without having to open them or pull them out from under the bed.

Buy clear watertight containers with lids that fit *into* your cooler for food storage. Combined they should take up about half the interior space of the cooler. These make storing fresh fruit, vegetables, cheese, olives, and other foodstuffs, *in your cooler*, easier. This also prevents them from getting soggy once the ice melts. Do not let fresh raw foods float in water. Heavy-duty zip lock bags can be used, but the plastic containers are more reliable.

You can carry firearms but the laws vary from state to state so I do not recommend them except as explained in detail in the **Security** chapter. A hammer is a better travel weapon. They are legal tools to carry and are not considered weapons when they are just stored under your seat or mattress. Choose one that is comfortable in your hand, one you can swing without dropping. Heavy hammers will make you easily lose your grip.

Carry a quality stainless steel folding locking knife. Keep a big one attached by your bed that you can find in the dark, and a small one with a blade less than 4" long that you can legally carry in your pocket while hiking. In some states, if the blade is less than 3" long, they are considered to be a utility tool when carried on your person rather than a concealed weapon.

I also recommend the special pepper spray system shown in the **Security** chapter to ward off both wildlife and human intruders. Carry these while hiking and while sleeping. In 20+ years of traveling I have never had to discharge or use any of them, but I like the peace of mind that comes from having them with me.

Security specialists state the two things you should do to protect something is first to hide it, and second to secure it. When carrying my laptop computer I devised a means of accomplishing both that seems to work well. My wife sewed pieces of matching material onto our seat covers. These *extensions* look like part of the original seat covers but hang down to

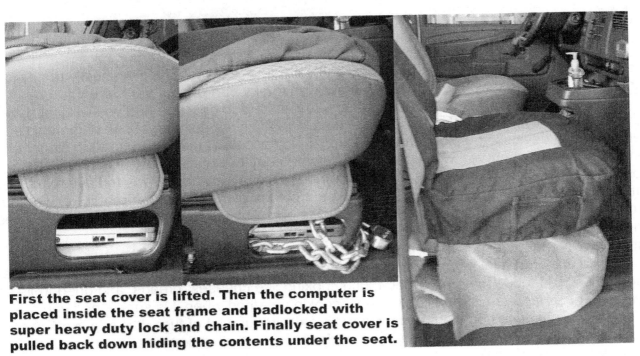

First the seat cover is lifted. Then the computer is placed inside the seat frame and padlocked with super heavy duty lock and chain. Finally seat cover is pulled back down hiding the contents under the seat.

the floor of the van. This covers the fact that I hide my computer *under the seat*. Then I wrap a massive chain around and through the seat frame and put a huge lock on it.

Even if a thief were to find it the computer cannot be pulled out of the small hole because it is now wrapped in chain. The first defense is most thieves do not know it is there. The second defense is they would have to work serious long handled bolt cutters from a very tight angle in order to cut anything due to the crowded location under the seat. See picture.

The next photo shows a heavy-duty *double-pronged* steering wheel lock we install when we are not present in the van. Use this kind of lock because it has two prongs on each end. This makes it more difficult to remove since cutting the steering wheel once will *not* allow

the device to be removed. It has been proven these deter thieves. Thieves usually target other vehicles when they see it installed. Never leave any part of your vehicle unlocked.

Food preparation is one of those things that is hard to describe and you will just have to work it out on your own. If you really like soups and canned dishes get one of the single serve heating devices you plug into your vans 12 volt accessory plug and heat up dinner or lunch whenever, wherever, with little fuss. They are easy to clean up too. The 12 volt oven described in the **FOOD** chapter is a good example. This is the easiest way to have a hot meal without breaking out the full kitchen or finding a crowded expensive restaurant for a two-hour ordeal when you'd rather be off exploring. Truck stops always have them for sale but the best ones can be found in the EQUIPMENT portion of the Vanabode Store (http://www.vanabode.com/camp/amazon-travel-store.htm).

We don't eat a lot of soup or canned food. We prefer raw foods like nuts, olives, fruits, vegetables, and foods that don't need much cooking like cheeses, breads, and dried fruits or cereals. The solar oven is the absolute best cooking method when it is sunny, and you are not in high winds, and you want to cook a big meal without a lot of fuss. It is super-efficient, requires no storage of dangerous fuels, is perfectly legal in all national parks where campfires or open grills are often illegal, and produces no smoke. With the sun oven you can cook anything you need up to 400 degrees for free, without electricity, smoke, fire, or fuel.

Combine a small camping stove, like the one shown in the **FOOD** chapter, with a propane fuel canister and a set of pots that fit on the stove's top for another great cooking solution. Get pots with sturdy handles and lids. Use a large metal stirring spoon and potholders to protect your hands. Deeper pots take up more room but we have found it surprisingly difficult to cook even a small quantity of food in a shallow pot.

Once my wife had just emptied the entire congealed contents of a can of corned beef hash into one of the shallow pots and it flipped right out slinky style. Our can shaped dinner rolled across the rubber van floor like a giant tootsie roll getting darker as it picked up every hair, piece of dirt and Bugsy residue it rolled over. After we got over the shock we both laughed until we cried. She then commenced to thoroughly wash it off and fed the entire one-pound can to me, refusing to eat any of it. Our dinner became *my* dinner. Deeper pots prevent this.

Get a good bed. There is no substitute for a good night's sleep. I purchased an expensive memory foam pillow top mattress. We sliced through the end of it and removed 3 rows of coils by cutting them out with wire cutters, making it a little shorter. Then my wife hand sewed the mattress cover back shut. Then I placed it on two sheets of plywood on top of two metal cabinets turned sideways across the back doors of the van. This enables us to sleep perfectly and store our plastic storage containers underneath. Some people prefer a slab of 4" to 6" foam. Foam is easier to install, cheaper, lighter, and quieter. But I prefer a first class spring mattress like the one I use in a house. Get the best you can afford because you will spend a third of your life there.

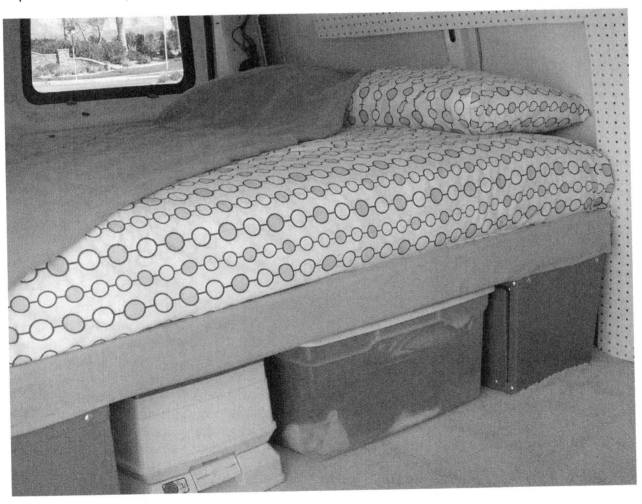

Other configurations are possible as well. You could stack bunk beds rack style against one wall. If you are over six feet tall you may wish to turn the bed so it runs long ways from front seat to back door. Mount it on a simple 2x4 frame with the plywood on top. This way you do not have to shorten the mattress at all and it allows for more normal exiting through the back doors. I prefer my way because it allows for more room in the middle of the van for toilet time, storing things, getting dressed, and fixing dinner, Cross ways allows us to both lay side by side and look out the back doors when the view is nice. See picture of our bed with storage underneath.

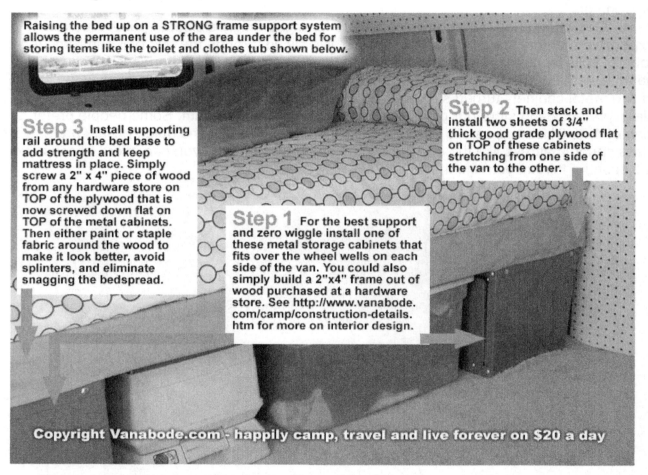

Raising the bed up on a STRONG frame support system allows the permanent use of the area under the bed for storing items like the toilet and clothes tub shown below.

Step 3 Install supporting rail around the bed base to add strength and keep mattress in place. Simply screw a 2" x 4" piece of wood from any hardware store on TOP of the plywood that is now screwed down flat on TOP of the metal cabinets. Then either paint or staple fabric around the wood to make it look better, avoid splinters, and eliminate snagging the bedspread.

Step 2 Then stack and install two sheets of 3/4" thick good grade plywood flat on TOP of these cabinets stretching from one side of the van to the other.

Step 1 For the best support and zero wiggle install one of these metal storage cabinets that fits over the wheel wells on each side of the van. You could also simply build a 2"x4" frame out of wood purchased at a hardware store. See http://www.vanabode.com/camp/construction-details.htm for more on interior design.

Buy two sets of high quality sheets. Get a 20 to 30 degree sleeping bag that unzips all the way open to use as a top blanket for cooler nights. We often happily hike all day in 70 degree weather in high elevations only to find the night temperatures in the 30 to 40 degree range. Without a sleeping bag over you the cold will ruin your night. Unable to sleep, time drags on, and the morning brings no relief because you will be more tired than when you first laid down. See the **Sleep** chapter for more on this issue and the van interior construction pages on the Internet (http://www.vanabode.com/camp/construction-details.htm).

Buy a good toilet. You cannot travel successfully without a properly designed and well-made portable toilet. The kind we use has a pull handle to drop the waste into a hidden tank below and seal it shut. It has a nice comfortable hinged seat.

The bottom holding tank disconnects. Then you can use the built in handle to carry it discretely into a building to empty (top portion of picture). We use a spray bottle to spray the bowl of the toilet down after each use.

The few times we have used the toilet for defecating we have put a small trash bag over the bowl lowered the seat, did our business, double bagged the excrement, then immediately disposed of it in a trash can. Otherwise you simply use the toilet anywhere, anytime, to urinate.

This makes it possible to stay inside all night without having to leave the van and without risking our privacy. Do not jeopardize your security by opening the doors in strange places to go outside at night to potty. See the **Personal Hygiene** chapter for more on this.

Privacy is important. Tint the windows as dark as you can. I highly recommend using the flat black, automatically expanding, fold out, automotive style, sunshade windshield covers for covering the windshield at night. These are quick to set up and take down and easy to store in the built in front door pocket. Get a set for the windshield and smaller ones for the side windows if you are not using a curtain inside.

With the back of the van dark at night most people look at the windshield and it just looks dark inside. They do not realize there is actually a cover on the inside and people sleeping behind it. This is how you stealth camp. You don't want to draw attention to your

vehicle when sleeping in a parking lot. It will look like a parked van, not one occupied by campers. This is why I do not recommend that you use the white pull curtain inside the van when in the city except for quickly changing clothes or using the toilet.

Coolers come in many configurations. Get a hard sided cooler; with a good quality drain plug, carrying handles, wheels, and a handle that extends for pulling behind you luggage style. Do not skimp on quality. A leaky plug will create headaches every day and a poorly insulated cooler will cost you a lot of extra money in ice. When you run out of ice, you end up spending a lot of time and burning a lot of gas running around buying ice everywhere.

A split lid enables you to open one side without opening the other and cup holders molded into the lid are nice. Make sure the cooler is sturdy enough to sit on as there are times you will need an extra seat. See the cooler picture.

Communication is very important to every person in your expedition. You should be able to reach all the others every time. Cell phones are the most popular solution.

However to save money, or if you are coming in from another country, you may find it much better to use the small, battery powered two way hand held radios for basic communication. They do not require cell phone towers and therefore do not typically have connectivity issues. There are no contracts required, they work up to a half-mile away, and they can be used when helping one another back up the van. I have found them helpful while using separate public restrooms to ensure safety.

Bicycles are *not* recommended while Vanaboding. There just aren't enough opportunities to use them. When you finally do get to use them they are often not as fun as simply walking. Over 80% of the trails in California, for instance, do not allow bicycles. Bicycles do provide another way of getting around. They can take you further in less time than walking, and can be great fun off road on wild trails and hills. However they cost you because they remove your ability to stealth camp. Securing them properly on the back of the van is a big hassle.

Our bikes and gear cost a total of $1600, and the helmets, the tire changing gear, the oils and locks, etc. take up room in the van. The rack we used to haul them cost $300, the hitch $120, and the 3 different kinds of locks with heavy chains designed to foil thieves $200. Still we worried about theft every time we left the van for a 3-4 hour activity and did not take the bikes with us. If you *love* biking then rig up like we did. If not leave them at home.

Bikes on racks draw unnecessary attention to your van. They make people think you are from out of town and camping, rather than just parking in the parking lot. All our long trips are done without the bikes. We do go on shorter "bike focused" trips where we ride every day in places dedicated to biking like Moab, Utah. These trips are focused solely on bike riding though so the extra work is worth it since the entire scene caters to bikers. The trails are set up for bikes, the towns have bike repair shops, and the locals talk the lingo. This makes hauling the bikes fun because you get to use them every day.

AAA memberships provide unlimited detailed color maps, trip routing, breakdown, and lockout service. If you run out of gas, break down or lock yourself out of your Vanabode they will come correct the problem at no charge. You simply call a toll free number from anywhere in the country. They also provide highly detailed topic specific maps like the California wine country maps that target the actual place you want to see rather than just giving you a bunch of connecting lines on a piece of paper. If you are traveling in a traditional recreational vehicle, camper, fifth wheel or travel trailer RV then do NOT use AAA. See my Good Sams information (http://www.rvforsaleguide.com/rv-links.htm) instead. Good Sams has much more for the recreational market and covers what AAA does not cover for RV's.

My Inventory list of what most people should use to Vanabode long term: Print this long paragraph and mark each item off as you acquire it. Polarized sunglasses help you see underwater when others see only glare. You need one or two heavy-duty plastic cups that fits into your vehicles cup holder for each person. Two long handled lighters for lighting the stove and making fire. Buy full sized toiletries like shampoo, conditioner, soap, and lotions which are then emptied into smaller containers for discreet public restroom use.

The advantages of a matching full size spare tire, not a donut, are outlined in the **Van** chapter. Maps from any source some of which can be downloaded and printed free from Google Maps. Get the most expensive air pump you can afford that can be powered by the cigarette lighter outlet or 12-volt outlet *and* powered with a normal house current plug (use the inverter while on the road). A pocket vest or jacket like the one shown previously to carry toothbrush, shaving cream, razor, wash cloth, and all other toiletries into convenience store bathrooms without getting hassled. I also use this on hikes where I want to carry lots of small items like binoculars, toilet paper, sun block, camera, and snacks, with or without a backpack. Plastic storage tubs sized to fit and stack under the bed without wasting space. In a pinch you can use one for bathing. Bottled drinking water with secure screw on caps, *not* the pull off type. Cheap gallon jugs of water or the super convenient heavy duty skinny 6 gallon BPA free jugs shown in the Vanabode Store (http://www.vanabode.com/camp/amazon-travel-store.htm) for drinking, bathing, washing dishes, and cleaning up. Refill them for free at gas stations or anywhere there is a water outlet. Fifty or more garbage bags and free grocery bags for garbage disposal. Bring smaller toilet sized plastic garbage bags if you want to defecate in the portable toilet. Newspaper helps with messy meal preparation and cleanup. When you are cutting up a huge juicy cantaloupe or honeydew on the cutting board the newspaper underneath catches all the runoff and can then be easily discarded. A heavy duty oven rack is good for putting over open campfires to rest food and pots on. Heavy cast iron skillets and pans, light black thin walled pots for use in the solar oven. Cooking utensil collection should include; a spatula, spoons, tongs, sharp knives, and oven gloves for hot campfire duties; one set of real silverware for each person, knives, forks, and spoons; a medium sized cutting board, don't get one too small or it will make a huge mess. Mine fits in a *shallow* cookie pan so I don't drip all over when cutting. You need a large bowl to mix foods in. Choose and bring either a liquid gas or propane grill and stove element burner. Bring a cooler with ice as described in previous chapters, a utility bucket to wash and store dishes in, dish washing detergent or liquid soap, small and medium sized flat rubber sink stoppers to use in public restrooms so you can shave, wash your hair, rinse clothes, or sponge off easily. Include two small kitchen towels and two sponges, old throw away towels in case of serious greasy van repairs, large beach towels for drying off after swim, covering up after a shower, and laying out at the beach instead of dragging the chairs or sleeping bags out. Thicker ones feel better but they take longer to dry. I recommend two thin ones per person. Bring two washcloths per person, use one while the other is drying, paper towels and plenty of toilet paper, a box of plastic eating utensils as a backup if the silverware is dirty, paper plates, paper bowls, and anything disposable. These make life easier since you do not need water to wash the dishes, or time to do dishes, or a place to store the dirty dishes in the meantime. Zip lock bags, both large and small, are among the most important convenience items. They are cheap and can be used for everything from storing sun block to storing food both in and out of the cooler. Baby wipes are very helpful for clean up without accessing your water supply along with waterless antibacterial hand wash. Bring a sun block product with SPF 50 or higher that you've tested on both face and body. Bring a flashlight with a compact strong beam of light and back up set of batteries, one sleeping bag that is rated down to 15-30 degrees for each person, or at least one to keep on the bed to use as a blanket for cold weather. Get the kind that unzip all the way and lay flat. Do not buy the mummy type. One compact, lightweight, folding, easy to store, lawn or camping chair for *each* person is essential. We wedge ours between the bed and the back doors. I highly recommend you test many chairs and pay whatever it costs to get the most comfortable chair that fits in your Vanabode easily. This one tool will make a huge difference in how well you relax and enjoy the outdoors while traveling. Use a breathable flexible bag for dirty clothes unless you prefer to store them in a tub under the bed. Bring at least 25 good quality bungee cords of various lengths, they will come in handy for everything from making a temporary clothesline to keeping things in place while driving rough terrain. To finish out this list I am again mentioning these which are detailed in previous places throughout this book: power inverter, cellular telephone, battery powered two way hand held radios for communication, thermometer with reliable dual indoor and outdoor readings, small hand held mirror, roof vent installed by a professional, clothes for all weather, wide brim hat, blank CD's and DVD's, DVD recorder, hammer, firearm if you like, pepper spray, knife, chain and lock for securing computer under the seat, solar oven, small camping stove attached to a propane fuel canister combined with a set of pots that fit on the stove's top, flat black automatically expanding fold out automotive style windshield cover, mattress, portable toilet. **OPTIONAL**: Small inflatable baby pool for bathing when no other options are available. Firewood stored in a plastic tub. I don't often do this since it can bring bugs in. A digital camera with an extra microchip to store images on until they are backed up, and a backup set of camera batteries.

The camping resources page (http://www.vanabode.com/camp/links.htm) and the Vanabode Store (http://www.vanabode.com/camp/amazon-travel-store.htm) have links to specialized discounted harder to find items. You can Vanabode easily and cheaply because most of what you don't already own, you can buy from these two online web pages I made for you for a few dollars, or in a pinch from Walmart.

Sample Itinerary

A **SAMPLE** Vanabode trips follows. Total miles driven = 4,218 with 74 - 141 total recommended days spent enjoying this adventurous route. To shorten this trip spend less time at any given place, skip some stopping points, or eliminate portions at either end. Get details on any of these places by visiting the destination pages online. (http://www.vanabode.com/travel/destinations.htm)

Remember the faster you drive the more money you spend. If you drive 30 miles a day you will only spend about $9 per day on fuel. If you spend a month in one spot like Yellowstone National Park you won't spend more than $50 on fuel in 30 days.

Carlsbad Caverns New Mexico, Mexican free tailed bats, extraordinary caves go for miles underground, it is so deep some people ride the underground elevator back up
2 Days spent, 304 miles to next destination, about a 5-7 hour drive

Albuquerque New Mexico, Sandia Peak Tramway, world's longest aerial tramway, great hikes, art galleries, nice place climate wise with some elevation making it cool
2 Days spent, 467 miles to next destination, about 9-12 hour drive

Grand Canyon National Park Arizona, hike, camp, ride mules, mind-boggling canyon rafting, and helicopter tours, you could easily stay here for the entire tourist season
2-6 Days spent, 130 miles to next destination, about 2-4 hour drive

Lake Powell Arizona Utah, do whatever it takes to get here, thousands of acres of stunning waterways and pristine free camping make this one of the most rewarding destinations in all of America. You **must** have or rent a boat, personal watercraft, canoe, or kayak to really enjoy it. You can beach camp here forever.
3-6 Days spent, 117 miles to next destination, about 2-4 hour drive

Zion National Park Utah, unforgettable, but a dangerous drive in for large motorhomes, Vanabode camping recommended, free shuttles to all hikes run all day
3-6 Days spent, 153 miles to next destination, about 3-5 hour drive

Las Vegas Nevada, most incredible city in the world, awesome food, shows, clubs, music scene, nightlife, and 15 acre pool complexes. There is no substitute for Las Vegas
5-15 days spent, 85 miles to next destination, about 2-3 hour drive

Death Valley, Badwater Basin, Artist's Drive, The Racetrack, sand dunes, spring fed swimming pool, don't go in the summer, winter season gets crowded but it is beautiful
3 Days spent, 70 miles to next destination, about 2-3 hour drive

China Ranch in Tecopa California, a real live desert oasis, date palm farm, desert arroyo hiking, canyons, rarely more than 15 people here at a time, very unique
1 day spent, 230 miles to next destination, about 5-7 hour drive

Joshua Tree National Park, spring and fall are the best times to enjoy this park; unbelievable rock formations and camping make for great peace and quiet
2-4 days spent, 254 miles to next destination, about 4 hour drive

Silver Strand State Beach California, pedestrian trail, grunions, lots of RV camping,
2-3 days spent, 5 miles to next destination, clean and pretty

Imperial Beach California, hosts annual U.S. Open Sandcastle Competition, interesting mix of people with lots of activity, clean and upbeat, not cheap
1 day spent, 5 miles to next destination

Tijuana Mexico, walk to another country but don't drink the water, no seriously do not drink the water, we were seriously ill for over a week because we were stupid. I no longer recommend anyone go into Mexico until they get the security corrected.

1 day spent, 17 miles to next destination, about 1 hour drive

San Diego California, San Diego Bay, Balboa Park, and San Diego Zoo, 15 museums, eight gardens, huge area that you could easily spend 3 months exploring

3 Days spent, 12 miles to next destination, about 1 hour drive

Mission Beach, the most popular beach in San Diego, fun, busy, good food joints and lots of pleasant people, upbeat, often sunny, above average to high prices for dinner

2 days spent, 2 miles to next destination

La Jolla Beach California, kayak, swim with seals, walk the cliff for long, scenic strolls, one of a kind beach scene, great for snorkeling, surfing, kayaking and relaxing

2 days spent, 2 miles to next destination

San Mateo Beach California, great campground with a trail leading to the beach, a lot of outdoor fun here, not too expensive for California, cold ocean water

2 days spent, 60 miles to next destination, about 1 hour drive

Los Angeles California, Griffith Park, Hollywood Boulevard, mall sized farmers market, Huntington Library has incredible art collections and botanical gardens, Los Angeles Arboretum and Botanic Garden is a massive 127 acres.

5 days spent, 30 miles to next destination, about 1 hour drive

Venice Beach California, gawk, shop, and stroll along the canals and beaches, great foods and hotels, pricey in places so shop around for lunch, quirky, funky

2 days spent, 2 miles to next destination

Santa Monica Beach California, the original muscle beach and street performers, day activities are great, expect a very colorful mix of people, safe fun

2 days spent, 18 miles to next destination

Malibu Beach California where films are shot and movie stars surf, great vibe, pay to park everywhere but still worth it, celebrity sightings

2 days spent, 86 miles to next destination, about 2-4 hour drive

Santa Ynez California Wine Trip, in the movie "Sideways", fun area, spread out

3 days spent, 135 miles to next destination, about 3-6 hour drive

Paso Robles California Wine Trip 150+ beautiful and friendly wineries, great town, my favorite wine destination in the United States for shear affordable variety

3-9 days spent, 42 miles to next destination, about 1-2 hour drive

Hearst Castle California, tour the magnificent historic castle, Neptune pool, I have never seen anything like this in an older dwelling or mansion, ticket prices vary widely

1-2 days spent, 230 miles to next destination, about 4-6 hour drive

San Francisco California, stunning city, great atmosphere, China Town, frogs in a bucket, world class food, eclectic population, bad drivers, never hot, often foggy, moody

5-20 days spent, 52 miles to next destination, about 1-2 hour drive

Point Reyes National Seashore California, Tule elk while walking Tomales Point Trail, super fun long hike with continuous extraordinary views along the way.

2 days spent, 33 miles to next destination, about 1 hour drive

Sonoma and Napa Valley California Wine Trip, beautiful estate wineries, upscale, expensive area, too expensive for my taste most of the time

3 days spent, 140 miles to next destination, about 3-4 hour drive

Mendocino Coast Botanical Gardens California, awesome dahlia blooming season, great gardens on ocean make this a very memorable place to visit. We will return. *2 days spent, 1082 miles to next destination, about 20-26 hour drive*

Yellowstone National Park Wyoming, huge wildlife scene, good camping, massive park, waterfalls and geyser water features, spend 2 months here if you can, dig in. *4-15 days spent, 455 miles to next destination, about 8-14 hour drive*

Montana - Glacier National Park, best rugged hiking and wildlife I have ever seen, I love this place, only open a few months a year, check everything before visiting. *4-20 days spent, from here you can head into Canada or anywhere else you like.*

Jason's Terms

I authored these definitions to describe difficult to understand principles that affect and govern our lives.

Possession Overload is the state most people find themselves in after purchasing a larger quantity of things than they can use or enjoy. They become sad, angry, depressed or frozen, unable to go anywhere or do anything new. Each purchase becomes a weight hanging about their neck instead of a pleasure.

Example *Illusion*: John believes if he buys the riding lawnmower he will have more time to go camping with his kids because he won't have to spend all weekend mowing the yard. *Reality*: John has to pay for the lawnmower, repair it, clean it, and store it. He has to buy a trailer to take it to the shop when it breaks down. This trailer must be stored, repaired, secured, licensed and cleaned as well. He gets fat from not mowing the yard with a traditional push mower and doesn't feel motivated to camp with his kids as much.

John then embraces the second *Illusion*: the television advertisement tells him if he buys a treadmill he will be able to get back in shape. *Reality*: John finds that walking the treadmill is even less fun than riding the lawnmower. He finds he is spending *even less time than ever camping with his children*. Now John is fatter, with less money in his bank account, has less room in his garage because he stores the riding lawnmower there, has less room in the yard because he stores the trailer there, has less room in his house because he stores the treadmill there, and is spending less time with his kids because he is busier than ever and more tired still.

John then buys a recliner so he can sit and rest and watch television. John is too tired to do anything else. From this soft boring seat he surveys the situation and realizes he has **Possession Overload**. He owns too much stuff that brings too little pleasure.

If the value of all your possessions is less than the *total cost of ownership* then you are in possession overload. People in this position are rarely ever able to Vanabode. The concept of admitting that all those purchases were mistakes and liquidating them at a further loss is too much for them to bear. So they stay put, do nothing, and make an even bigger mistake than the previous one. They cost themselves their life.

Duped Consumer is a person tricked into a purchase they end up not enjoying because they did not understand the *total cost of ownership* in terms of time and money when they made the purchase.

Example *Illusion*: when Tom bought the boat all he could see was his wife in her bikini on the bow and his children fishing happily off the stern. *Reality*: Tom got very tired very fast working the extra job to make the boat payment, pay the taxes, make the repairs, do the maintenance, pay for storage, buy insurance and make equipment upgrades.

Illusion: Tom thought he would be able to take the boat out every week for a nice long weekend. *Reality*: Tom was too tired to go every weekend, sometimes the kids were sick, sometimes the wife had planned something else, sometimes the weather was bad, sometimes the boat was in the shop, and sometimes Tom had to work. Tom ended up using the boat for about 12 days a *year* during major holidays when he could get off work.

Analyze the Alternative is a thought process for analyzing the consequences of *not* proceeding with a strange new idea, like Vanaboding. You can come up with many excuses why you cannot travel for a year. Usually these excuses are just a cover for laziness. The very things you are hoping to protect by *not* proceeding are actually the ones being lost.

Example: some people fear not having enough money to take care of themselves when they get old so they save every dime they make and rarely do anything fun or worthwhile because it would be too expensive. Guess what? You probably won't have enough money to take care of yourself whether you stay home or not! *Analyze the alternative* to taking a chunk of savings and living it up for a year. Compare Vanaboding to huddling up in your house. As I demonstrate in the **Budget** chapter people spend more money living at home than you do Vanaboding! That's a fact!

Conclusion: you can live longer and more happily while on a well-planned Vanabode trip than you can by any other method. So staying home to save money is a mistake. Hasn't the troubling collapse of 2008-2010 taught us anything? People are losing everything they have, not because of the *bad* economy, but because they live paycheck to paycheck, and NEVER save a dime. Within a month or two of job loss they immediately lose everything else as well. *Conclusion*: staying home to save money is an illusion. It is illogical. It does not work. Many people save more money while traveling and living the Vanabode lifestyle than they do housebound.

Romance Wasting describes what happens when you try to do something fun and romantic but because you do not have enough time to really settle in and experience everything at your destination, you instead come away feeling jaded, tired, and very unfulfilled. Despite what the travel agent tells you time is the single greatest element to having a good complete experience anywhere, not money.

Example: You plan all year for a pathetic 5-7 day vacation hoping to cram in a wonderful romantic cruise with our spouse. You scrimp and save all your pennies just to afford a one-week cruise. You rush to get to the airport and then to the cruise port eating up your first day entirely. You pinch pennies while on the cruise because your normal lifestyle does not allow for much additional savings beyond the initial air and cruise tickets. Half way through the week it starts raining. Huddled up in a hotel room, with dumb programs playing on the television, it all of a sudden just feels like the same old story. Bored, and realizing this is it, that there are no more fun days for another year, lovers begin to blame each other.

Arguments brew. Discontentment evolves into shame. Fear that life is disappearing comes over you both. Finally, the sun comes out, and you spend the last day sipping an overpriced cocktail, hiding under an umbrella to keep from getting more sunburned than you already are.

The next day, back on your job, grinding out the hours, you realize that most of the time you were not *present* on your vacation. You were either sleeping, going to and from the cruise, stuck watching television, fielding phone calls from the office, answering emails on day to day nothings, or posing for awful pictures you will later upload to Facebook to show all your digital friends the great time you had.

Everybody knows it is all a lie though. We've all been down this road before. We have all wasted the romance when we thought we could buy with money from a travel agency what only *extended periods of time can provide*. We all stumble into that terrible day at some point; when we realize we have so few days left to do the things we dream about; having wasted so much time on nothing.

Prioritize Your Pleasure - You must *prioritize your pleasure* in order to have FUN because the world is too complicated and our lives are too busy to expect fun to take care of itself. See more on this in the **Fun** chapter.

Jason's Travel Heritage

I invented the Vanabode lifestyle. "But do I live it?" You ask. "Yes I do". My wife and I have traveled thousands of miles all over the United States. We have van, RV and truck camped in almost every state and national park in America. We have been up and down both coasts. We know what it feels like to be cramped in a car, or unable to enter an interesting place because our motor home is too big. We learned the best way to have a fun American life is to Vanabode.

We have been married 18+ years now and have gone through many stages of Vanaboding. In our early years we took 4-day weekends every month because we were working too much to go any longer. We were not satisfied. We started taking more time off from work. Sometimes this made the relationship with our employers very uncomfortable. However, we made special arrangements to get 4-5 weeks at a time off to take longer more adventurous trips. It was during these extraordinary early journeys that we realized neither of us would ever be happy if we only sporadically traveled short-term. We also realized that we did not have enough money to travel on longer trips. In order to continue we would need more money.

At first we did everything wrong. We planned and endlessly schemed for days off from our typical jobs. Then when we finally got time off we ended up driving too many miles, trying to see so much in the little time we had. We broke the *prioritize your pleasure* element of the Essentials of a Great Life. We didn't eat well because we didn't know how. We broke the *excellent food* element of the *Essentials of a Great Life.* We never got the kind of sleep we needed because we didn't know how to get a good night's sleep on the road. We broke the *great sleep* element of the *Essentials of a Great Life.* The list goes on and on.

Basically we were doing the same thing everyone else was doing. It was all wrong. It was impractical, expensive and unfulfilling. It was not sustainable. Since the American Plains Indians were killed off and most of their lands taken, the art of living freely here in America has virtually died. Now very few people know how to live unencumbered. We certainly didn't.

At first I was very depressed. This is a sign of mental illness. Living this unfulfilling 9-5 life was making my brain sick! I really got motivated when I found a secret NASA document that proves for every ONE year past the age of 55 worked, the average person sacrifices TWO years of their life because they die earlier. Work kills! (http://www.marketingmakesmoney.com/work-longer-die-younger.htm)

So I came up with a plan. I got rid of time constraints by getting rid of my job. I got rid of my job by getting rid of my debt. I got rid of my debt by not buying things I didn't need. I stopped buying things I didn't need when I had more fun without them.

We worked hard and paid off all our debts. We sold our second car. We sold our townhome and two others we had bought as investments. We sold everything except major furniture, gifts, photo albums and things of sentimental value. Everything else went into storage.

My children were living with their mother at the time so I offered to take them with us and home school them while on the road. They did not want to go. We left Florida and traveled for years, returning to Florida every 4 months or so to cover holidays with my children, the extended family, and our friends. For many years my children lived and traveled with us during the summers when they were out of school.

We could not travel forever on my savings alone so I uncovered a way to make a little money every day from anywhere in the world, freeing us up to travel without a job or employer. If you are interested in making money this way to support your lifestyle check out the Resource Page (http://www.vanabode.com/camp/quit-your-job-make-money.htm). It is not hard to do and you too can make money forever this way. Having money flowing in, with very little flowing out, makes you feel powerful. This is exactly how I got into trouble.

The banks liked what I was doing even though I didn't have a pay stub. If you are debt free they want to loan you money. So I got the brilliant idea to buy a condo in Vegas where we spend a few months every year. Las Vegas is a perfect base camp for taking 2-4 month trips all over the West. Then when the value went straight up I thought, "Well I can make money like everyone else by buying yet another house and renting the condo out". Wrong.

Boom! The housing market crashes and I am back to wishing I had followed my own advice and stayed *free* of mortgages and just Vanaboded. We all learn our lesson one way or another. Even when I knew what to do: simply Vanabode happily forever, I let the same greed that has overcome the world, overtake me as well. Sad. Do not let this happen to you. Stay free, get out and about, and avoid the pain I brought on myself.

Many of the places we have visited are listed in the free Destination Guides online. (http://www.vanabode.com/travel/destinations.htm) Some places are not worth mentioning. Others we have kept a secret for ourselves. You can do the same. You can find extraordinary interesting places to live in, vacation in, or camp at, by following the simple affordable plans I have outlined. Reengineer your life to reclaim your time, enable more travel, and reduce stress from excessive debts and responsibilities.

Vanabode Extras for Customers Only

FREE Updates Forever as long as you are on the email list: I will be updating this book for the rest of my life. Updates are FREE forever to anyone that has purchased my book at any time. As we travel the United States we will continue to add Destination pages so you can have instant updated information on thousands of new places to see and enjoy. Of course each comes complete with pictures, navigation advice, temperature information, safety, and GPS coordinates when necessary. Request to be on my mailing list (http://www.vanabode.com/contact.htm) so I can send you the free updates.

Vanabode Network (http://www.vanabode.com/camp/airbnb-vanabode-network.htm) consists of thousands of homeowners and business owner hosts. These hosts agree to allow Vanaboders hassle free overnight parking stays at a super low rate sometimes for as little as $4. This allows individuals all over the United States to make a few bucks and meet interesting people. In return Vanaboders get a safe proven place to park knowing for sure there will be no overnight hassles. Some of these hosts act as little bread and breakfast establishments allowing outdoor shower or bathroom use, while some leave you to yourself.

Income: I will pay anyone providing a **Destination Report** for reprint rights so I can add it to the Vanabode Destination Guide (http://www.vanabode.com/travel/destinations.htm)

Important Long Term Travel Resources

Destinations Guide contains hundreds of our trip reports and thousands of pictures.
http://www.vanabode.com/travel/destinations.htm

Quit your job make money while traveling shows 25+ ways to earn a living while camping and traveling as well as how to find hundreds of jobs for seasonal campers.
http://www.vanabode.com/camp/quit-your-job-make-money.htm

New Vanabode Web Pages contains links to **new pages not contained in the book**
http://www.vanabode.com/camp/sitemap.htm

Important external websites supporting Vanabode living and travel. Links include the "spring finder" for finding fresh free water bubbling out of the ground, and the "farmers market finder" for locating 1000's of organic farmers markets selling roadside, and links to climate resources for all temperature and weather data on where you will be camping for every month of every year, and the master "host list" displays hidden communities all over the United States that welcome you to park and live in exchange for a little labor or expertise. You will find other links to book and equipment vendors that I recommend. These links cover a variety of topics like: where to camp for free, how to how to hide your money and disappear, maps, specialized van ready equipment, cameras, camping clubs, and products to save you money. One site offers a special $180 permit that gets you a camping spot for 7 months.
http://www.vanabode.com/camp/links.htm

RV for Sale Guide as a recognized travel authority in the United States I provide discussions of everything RV, camping, and motorhome related including *where* to travel
http://www.rvforsaleguide.com

BLM Free Camping official government website shows millions of acres of free camping
http://www.blm.gov

Vanabode Forum, be part of the network of off grid travelers, post and see pictures, profiles, questions and answers, designed to help you stay in touch with your extended family.
http://forums.vanabode.com

Amazon Special Camping Store showcases books and equipment for cheap Vanaboding
http://www.vanabode.com/camp/amazon-travel-store.htm

My Real Vegas and A Las Vegas Deal contain my personal insider information on Vegas hotels, airfare, casinos, clubs, shows, parties, wedding packages, golf, and shopping.
http://www.myrealvegas.com and http://www.alasvegasdeal.com

Bus for Sale Guide I created this for those interested in travel by bus or RV conversion.
http://www.busforsaleguide.com

Maintain a Relationship with God

If you don't know God, you will never be *completely* satisfied with your life. Dying is a hell of a time to not believe in God. While living is no fun either. All the lost share these characteristics: they are empty, lonely, guilty, and afraid of death.

This is not a religious book. However, whether Vanaboding or not, if you are addressing all the *Essentials of a Great Life*, and are *still* not satisfied, it's because you lack a good relationship with God. Find a local Christian church that teaches the entire bible. Then seek forgiveness through the sacrifices God made by sending his son Jesus Christ to die for your sins. This will serve to reestablish your relationship with God and allow the two of you to get to know each other.

During the times over the years that I struggled with my Christianity and faith in God, I realized this important truth. There is no lifestyle on earth that is so much more enjoyable than the one I lead as a Christian, that it is worth taking the chance there is no God to live it.

Email me (http://www.vanabode.com/contact.htm) if you want to. I will be glad to help.